THE ADVENTUROUS LIVES OF

THE GREAT EXPLORERS

A LOOK AND LEARN—WORLD OF WONDER BOOK

Pictured here is a caravel, a type of sailing vessel in common use during the 15th century, by explorers like Vasco da Gama and Christopher Columbus.

Hilary Masson

CONTENTS

'Published by IPC Magazines Ltd., Fleetway House, Farringdon Street, London, England. Sole Agents for Australia and New Zealand: Gordon & Gotch Ltd; South Africa: Central News Agency Ltd; Rhodesia and Zambia: Kingstons Ltd. Printing by Stabilimento Tipolitografico G. Canale & C. Torino (Italy)'.

JOHN HANNING SPEKE

SUN SCORCHED TREK TO THE BASIN OF THE NILE

John Hanning Speke had a burning belief that he had solved one of the oldest mysteries of Darkest Africa. Risking ridicule and contempt he made his way back to prove his point . . .

The sun was burning into the young Englishman's skin with such fierce, scalding pain that he wanted to lie down and scream. Thirst seemed long ago to have bleached the last drop of moisture from his mouth and throat, and planted there a tongue that felt like cracked parchment.

Weariness had hours since set trembling each nerve and muscle in his body till his every step was a separate agony.

A glance at his companion in that cruel cauldron of burning Africa, reinforced his will to keep going. "I'm hanged if I'll complain," he thought. "If he can stay the pace, so shall I!"

John Hanning Speke had already called on his body for too many reserves of stamina, but now he demanded extra. Though he disliked the discomfort, he disliked his companion, the fiery-tempered and arrogant explorer, Richard Francis Burton, even more.

The two men were in Somalia, and this was Speke's first experience of Africa—the Dark Continent, as it was known then in 1854—but it was an experience for which Speke himself had pleaded. That was one of the reasons why he would show no sign of his personal torment.

The two men already had seen too many hardships that few others would have survived. They had stalked warily through waving savannah in which lurked deadly beasts of prey, plodded wearily on across seemingly endless torrid plains and hacked out tracks through matted, clinging jungle where deadly humidity soaked a man in rivulets of perspiration, draining his will to live.

They had encountered marauding Arabs and hostile black warriors, sat awake through terrifying nights, peering into the eerie shadows for the sudden movement or sound of a cracking twig that might suggest hunters were upon them.

Speke had been wounded, taken prisoner, tortured and rescued with only the greatest daring.

And, as if those were not trials enough, he and Burton disliked each other intensely. It was almost as though they had been born not to understand each other—Speke, reserved and quiet, somewhat fanciful in his ways with the air of an aristocrat; Burton bursting with brashness, harsh and hard, from a very ordinary background.

Why did this fever for exploration grip John Hanning Speke of all people?

When he was born on 3rd May, 1827, it seemed likely that most of his life would be spent around the quiet countryside of Bideford in Devon. Tiny, peaceful pools, gently flowing rivers and the leafy, friendly woods that skirted his birthplace seemed to fit the quiet young boy's character.

Perhaps Speke's first journey overseas awakened the desire to see bigger and bolder landscapes. After a somewhat rigorous education, he became a cadet in the Anglo-Indian Army at the age of seventeen. Fighting in India, he soon became a captain, only to discover that it was not warfare that had taken grip of his interest. He preferred travel, as journeys across the Himalayan boundaries and through Tibet revealed to him.

In 1854, he was introduced to Burton in Aden—and at that moment, impressed immensely by the great explorer, he knew he had to follow in his restless footsteps.

So it was in Somalia that he found himself—facing the most torturous experience and, moreover, the realisation that he disliked this man whom he had at first admired so much. To make things even worse, Burton's expedition to Somalia turned out to be a failure.

Sadder but wiser, Speke returned to Devon where he spent his time hunting and studying natural sciences. Perhaps he was destined after all for the quiet life.

Unknown to him, however, events were already in motion that were to have the profoundest effect on his life.

In London, the British Royal Geographical Society was in session. Its members had long been turning their eyes towards what was believed to be one of the longest rivers in the world. And now they were setting themselves an enormous task—to discover the source of the river: *the Nile*.

For long hours they debated, finally deciding the ideal starting point for such a journey would be Zanzibar, the nearest point to the mysterious heart of the Black Continent.

Only one more decision remained to be made. Who would lead the expedition? Richard Francis Burton was their man.

Soon afterwards John Hanning Speke received one of the most startling surprises of his young life. Burton wanted him as his companion on the expedition.

It seemed too incredible to be true. When they had parted last, their paths looked like never crossing again. But Burton's invitation was clear enough. Speke agreed delightedly—and thought that perhaps their differences could be settled this time.

Bagamoyo was a tiny place on the mainland facing Zanzibar, and it was from here that Burton and Speke set out on 27th June, 1857, trekking steadily onwards for five months until they reached the village of Kazeh, an Arab trading post.

At once they started to make inquiries and learned of three large lakes which lay to the West and South-West—lakes known today as Tanganyika, Victoria and Nyasa.

One of those three lakes might well be the enormous natural reservoir from which tumbled the Nile.

By now both Burton and Speke were in bad health, but fired with fresh determination to accomplish their aim, they set out from Kazeh on a march that was to last two months. Exhaustion held them back, optimism pushed them on. But how their minds must have hoped and begged that over every crest they might finally see the great lake they sought!

Suddenly it was there. Burton and Speke stood on the shore

On 21st July, 1862, John Hanning Speke pointed ahead excitedly. There before him snaked the winding Nile.

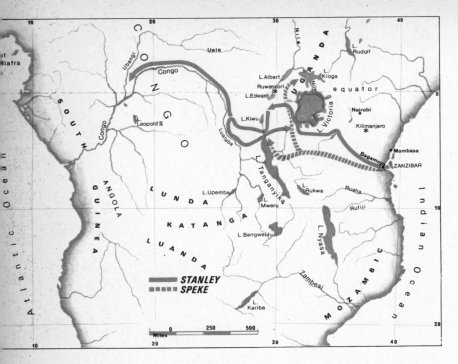

Crocodiles basked in the sun, hippopotami frolicked in the waters and flocks of birds swooped over the lush vegetation.

of an immense lake in which blue, peaceful waters lapped lazily against its meandering perimeter.

"We shall call it Tanganyika," said Burton, adopting its local name, and then he set about charting its position and determining its height. In his mind was no doubt that he had discovered the source of the Nile. Where else could it start?

Certain that his mission was accomplished, Burton decided to return to Kazeh where, in ill health, he began to write the report of his success. And at that point there started another controversy between the two explorers.

John Hanning Speke had been thinking carefully during the return to Kazeh, and he did not feel convinced that Lake Tanganyika was the starting point of the Nile.

According to his calculations, Lake Tanganyika was situated less than ten feet higher than the Nile at Gondokoro, just over 700 miles to the north.

That meant the great river was falling only about ten feet in a distance of over 700 miles. The very idea was impossible. There had to be another basin at a greater height, one that would give the water greater impetus at the start of such a long journey.

What was more, the natives had spoken of *three* lakes. One was too far to the south, so that was certainly out of the question. But what about the other?

Leaving Burton in Kazeh, Speke set out with a few men and made his way back into the heart of Africa. And on 30th July, 1858, after an uneventful journey, he finally sighted a hill behind which there was the great lake.

Speke's delight knew no bounds. This was it. This was the real basin of the Nile. He felt certain of it.

Hastily he returned to Kazeh and told Burton of his discovery and conclusions. The Nile had to flow from that lake—which Speke had named Lake Victoria in honour of his queen—and not from Lake Tanganyika which was far too low.

Burton listened gloomily. If what Speke said was true, his own journey and observations had been of very little value.

"Yours is not a scientific conclusion, Speke", he replied coldly. "It is no more than an inspiration."

The atmosphere between the two men could have been cut with a knife. Speke glared contemptuously at his companion, fixing him with a withering stare. Burton returned the look defiantly before turning away with a slight sneer.

Now neither wanted to break the embarrassed silence that followed the conversation. Furthermore, they were both sick, and anxious to return home, a journey they started soon afterwards, reaching the coast in February, 1859, and sailing then for Aden.

Burton decided to remain there for a while to cure his malaria, but Speke left immediately for England. However, he promised his companion he would await his arrival in London before revealing the results of the expedition.

Speke, though, knew it would be difficult to keep such a promise. His conclusions were only a guess, true—but he felt he was right. The glory of discovering the source of the Nile was within easy grasp. How could he possibly give it up?

He did not. Visiting the President of the Royal Geographical Society, Speke told him all about the expedition, explained his conclusions, passionately declared his certainty, and finally asked if he might organise another trip—the final one—to the source of the Nile.

The Royal Society had many doubts, and aired them, but finally gave its grudging consent to help him. While Burton, bitter, irritated and disappointed was returning to England, Speke was already on his way back to Africa.

With him this time was an old friend from his days in India, James Grant—and on 25th September, 1860, heading an expedition of several hundred native bearers and guides, they left Bagamoyo, reaching Kazeh four months later.

Months were spent waiting to hear from Suwarora, chief of the Usui, months that seemed interminable and agonising in lands that were hostile and uncomfortable and where the natives could be all too treacherous and murderous.

But finally on 4th October, 1861, a messenger from Suwarora brought the long-awaited permission to cross his territory. Speke and Grant were on their way again.

On the 17th December, they were forced to halt once more. They had now reached the boundaries of Karaghé territory. At once a messenger was dispatched to the court of Mtesa, all-powerful king of Uganda.

Speke hoped and hoped. He knew only too well that without permission from Mtesa, the expedition might as well pack up and go home. The Ugandan chieftain's reputation had spread far and wide. He was said to be cruel, of wicked temper and inclined to kill men merely to satisfy a whim.

It was 8th January, 1862, when the frantic beating of drums heralded the arrival of a caravan, led by an envoy from Mtesa.

Solemnly he announced that his king was prepared to offer his hospitality to white men, whom he had never seen before, and he wished them to go to him without delay.

As Grant was sick at the time and could not be moved, Speke reluctantly had to leave him behind. "But meet me as soon as possible at the court of Mtesa," he said to his companion. Both men wondered if they would ever see each other again.

Speke packed away his instruments after calculating the height of the Nile above sea level. Now he felt certain that Burton was wrong.

Speke had to confess his surprise as he travelled through Mtesa's territory. It was green and fertile, slightly hilly and the climate was mild. But what impressed him most were the well-made tracks, the large, tidy villages, beautifully-kept gardens and well cultivated fields. It was a new and exalting aspect of Africa.

"Finally, on 19th February, a day's march brought us close to the royal palace of Uganda," the explorer wrote in his diary. But not until the following day was Speke admitted to the presence of Mtesa.

"The powerful monarch was sitting on his throne in the ceremonial hut. I therefore advanced with my hat in my hands."

Mtesa remained in the shade as one of his dignitaries advanced and indicated to Speke to stop. The explorer sat on a folding chair he had taken with him. No one spoke.

A few moments passed, and Speke felt the equatorial sun beating down its searing heat on to his head. He opened the umbrella he had with him. The crowd murmured stupefied. Then there was silence again while the two men—the black king and the white explorer—stared at each other.

For a whole hour nothing happened. Then Mtesa ordered an interpreter to say something to Speke.

"His Majesty asks if you have seen him."

"For an hour I have had this pleasure", answered the explorer. At this reply Mtesa stood up and walked away. Speke thought he had offended him but was reassured that the king was simply going to eat and would gladly receive him afterwards.

Speke stayed with Mtesa till July; and he saw for himself that what he had heard about the young king was true. His first proof of the sovereign's eccentric cruelty came when Mtesa loaded a rifle he had just received as a present.

"He gave it to a page, ordering him to go and kill a man in the nearby courtyard," wrote Speke.

On 27th May, several shots announced the arrival of Speke's companion, Grant, now in fairly good health, though still walking with great difficulty. And it was then that Speke asked Mtesa for permission to leave; though the King would not grant it until July.

One of his better whims eventually came to the fore. He ordered some of his own men to join the expedition to help it along and give any assistance they could. On 7th July, 1862, Speke and Grant left under a fierce sun.

Their march continued for about ten days without incident, but the pace was slow. Grant, in fact, was being tortured by acute pains in his legs. It was impossible to continue.

So once more the two companions agreed to separate. Speke was to press on to the Nile and then track back to its source. Grant was to make his way to the kingdom of Unyoro to try to establish good relations with its chieftain, Kamrasi, whose help they needed for the return journey.

Above them towered the mighty waterfall that tumbled from Lake Victoria.

On 19th July, the caravan split. Grant went west while Speke took the opposite direction, where he hoped to solve the ancient enigma for all time.

After a hard and tiring march, the young explorer reached the shores of the great river on 21st July.

"Here I am, here I am at last, on the shores of the Nile", his diary records. "Nothing is more beautiful than the sight before me.

"Crocodiles bask in the sun while others move in the high grass on the banks. There in the trees, herds of antelopes wander, while hippopotami spurt water from their nostrils, and at every step flocks of birds fly from under our feet."

The following day, 22nd July, he went up-stream with a few companions to the last stretch of the Nile.

As though some unseen benevolent fate was now smiling on the expedition, all the pitfalls and perils of the journey seemed to vanish. The tropical diseases, the deadly stings of the insects, the arrows of the hostile natives, every danger and every anxiety seemed to stay away from the party.

Suddenly Speke pricked up his ears. First faintly, then louder and louder, he heard the thunder of a waterfall.

Speke stumbled on, quickening his pace through the last stretches of jungle—and at last the waterfall was there.

"There was the thundering of the water, the jumping of the migrant fish, the fishermen in boats lying in wait with fishing lines on every rock, the hippopotami and the crocodiles, and up above the falls the herds, come to drink at the lakeside."

Speke was fascinated and greatly moved. "Our expedition had achieved its purpose." It was 26th July, 1862.

Speke baptised the falls with the name of the President of the Royal Geographical Society, Ripon; and he would have liked, in the next few days, to have explored the lake's shores and the surrounding territories. But he was unable because of the stubborn refusal of Mtesa's men.

Then Grant reached the camp, limping, disappointed and worried. Kamrasi, King of Unyoro, would not allow him to cross the frontiers into his kingdom.

But these difficulties with Kamrasi—and others—were overcome one by one, and the two explorers together managed to make an adventurous journey back.

In summer, 1863, Speke sent from Khartoum to London and to the world his famous cable: 'The Nile is done with."

Back home, honours awaited him. Ceremonies, rewards and recognition were his for the taking . . . but there were controversy and bitterness to face too.

Burton, who had not forgiven Speke for what he had done and said to him three years before, challenged him to a debate before the Royal Geographical Society.

Speke accepted calmly, and while waiting for the confrontation, lived peacefully in his quiet house in Devon where, for about a year, he worked on his memoirs and on his collections, every now and then hunting in the misty countryside.

It was during one of these hunting trips—on 21st September, 1864, that a shot fired accidentally from his own gun struck him full blast. He was dying before he hit the ground.

John Hanning Speke, who had challenged one of the last secrets of Africa—who had revealed the time-old mystery of the source of the Nile—had been deprived by cruel and ironic fate of his final triumph which he justly and rightly deserved . . . triumph over the man who had mocked him.

For a whole hour Speke sat motionless before the bloodthirsty African tyrant king. One false move or word, and he knew his life might be ended.

GIOVANNI DA PIAN DEL CARPIN

Halfway across the unknown world
rode a fat little friar on a donkey...

INTO THE STRONGHOLD OF THE MERCILESS MONGOLS

"Aye, well, perhaps now we shall settle an argument once and for all," growled the strong, burly knight to his companion. "Perhaps we shall see at last whom his Holiness considers the bravest knight in Christendom. And t'is a brave man indeed he'll have to be to dare make his way into the stronghold of those savage Mongols!"

Knights and noblemen from all parts of the civilised Christian world waited expectantly at the court of Pope Innocent IV. All of them knew that the foundations of their civilisation had been rocked greatly by the savage, sweeping attacks of a deadly foe from the East. And all of them knew that the Pope now meant to send someone into those territories.

But which man? That was the question on everyone's lips. Surely he must be the bravest of the brave, a warrior more fearless than any in that dawn of the 13th century?

"He comes! He comes!" The cry echoed from wall to wall, and every neck craned forward, every eye strained harder for a first glimpse of this man who had been summoned to tread the first frightening path into the unknown Eastern lands of the cruel and merciless Mongols.

Astonishment and a mounting murmur of amazement greeted the appearance of the Pope's chosen ambassador.

Towards the court rode not a fine knight in splendid armour on a magnificent charger, but a roughly dressed friar, rather old and grey-bearded, and so fat that he could not mount a horse but rode a donkey.

"The good God help us," muttered one knight to another. "Has his Holiness taken leave of his senses that he sends to these savages not the very fearless but the very fattest?"

Giovanni da Pian del Carpine rode through the gathered throng without a word, dismounted and waddled to the chambers of the Pope. Although he understood the grave dangers of his mission, no fear betrayed its presence on his kindly face. He was fully prepared to die for the Cross and Christianity—and probably would.

The eyes of the two men met, and in them probably were framed understanding and awareness of the many risks ahead—and also remembrance of the flood of Mongol terror that had poured across the world like a torrent of blood.

Long ago an astrologer had foretold the arising of a 'great tempest' on 16th September, 1188. But it was not to the weather the prophet had referred. That night a 'great tempest' had arisen—with the birth of Genghis Khan, the Mongol who laid waste to half the world.

He began to build a powerful empire in the East, a task that took him less than twenty years. And then he turned his eyes towards the West. Christendom was now to know the name of Ghenghis Khan and never to forget it.

Neither city wall nor fortified castle was defence against the Mongols. Small men mostly, with skins like yellowed olives and eyes that burned cruelly, they raced into battle, leather-clad, on fast, tiny horses. When their deadly arrows had done their work, the bloodthirsty hordes would race in search of other victims, leaving behind them charred and smoking ruins among which lay the dead and dying.

Even when Genghis Khan died in 1227, there was no halt. Still the Mongols forced and fought their way onwards, crushing opposition like so many handfuls of flies in a fist.

Russia was almost completely overrun. Hungary trembled before them and was ravaged. Panic swept across Germany.

Together Polish and German warriors faced the Mongols at Liegnitz on 9th April, 1241 and tasted only the bitterest defeat. Now, it seemed, the world could only pray.

If it did, its prayers were answered; for the Mongols elected to fall back to Russia for a time and give their armies a rest.

In the West, however, the nightmare was by no means ended. The whole of Christian Europe wondered how long it would be before the Mongols came again.

But what added most to their fears was how little they knew of these conquerors.

Surrounded by fierce Mongol warriors, the brave friars were escorted to the camp of General Cortensa.

L. ARCAS -70

From where exactly did they come? Where was the capital of their great empire? And now, if Genghis Khan was dead, who wore the crown in his place?

There were other mysteries that demanded explanation. These Mongols—known too as Tartars—had also attacked Moslem towns and fortresses. Moslems were still the sworn enemies of Christianity. So what did it all mean?

Was it that, like Christians, the Mongols were religious rivals and enemies of Islam? Or was it simply that they wished war with every foreigner, whatever his faith?

There was one thing only about which everyone was certain —the inhuman cruelty of the Mongols.

Russian, Hungarian, Polish and German armies, when captured, had been killed by atrocious tortures. Whole towns had been destroyed. Thousands of men, women and children had been beheaded or stabbed to death. And it was said that the Mongols burned the lands they conquered, even swamping them with salt to destroy their fertility forever.

Was there any possibility of reaching an understanding with the Mongols? Was negotiation a possibility? Could any compromise be reached?

Obviously there was but one way to find out. Someone had to venture into their empire—to talk to them, see their towns, study their customs, explore their land—and report back.

Now it was known that the chosen ambassador of the Pope was a fat friar on a drooping donkey.

To this day no one is certain when or where Giovanni da Pian de Carpine was born—though it was probably towards the end of the 12th century in a small town today called Magione, not far from Lake Trasimeno in Umbria, Italy.

When he first felt his calling to the Church is unknown, too, but it was to the Order of Minor Friars that he was attracted.

Nearer to the court of Kuyuk Khan they came, the falling snow making their journey more unbearable.

Soon after, he became one of the earliest and most enthusiastic followers of Saint Francis of Assisi, one of the most remarkable men of his age.

In 1221, Giovanni was sent to Germany to spread the teachings of the saint. Then, at the time when the Mongols began to organise themselves in the conquered territories of Russia, Giovanni was appointed Guardian of the Province of Saxony. In 1228, the year after the death of Genghis Khan, he assumed responsibility for the whole province of Germany.

He would send missions to Hungary, to Bohemia and to Denmark, and he made it a point to learn the various languages of Central Europe. He travelled to Spain and then returned to Italy. Later, he went to Poland.

It was because of his knowledge of Central Europe and all the information he had collected about the Mongols that the Pope entrusted to him the delicate and dangerous mission of going right into the heart of their kingdom.

A man free from earthly interests, prepared to die a martyr if needs be and, above all, one whose words would be sincere— such was the ambassador whom Pope Innocent IV wished to confront the barbaric Mongols.

On 16th April, 1245, Giovanni took possession of some letters from the Pope addressed to the Great Khan. Then, with another friar, Stephen of Bohemia, and a few servants, he left Lyon to face whatever fate held in store for him.

The early part of the journey held few problems or terrors. Giovanni took roads that he knew well, roads that crossed Europe towards the East. In Prague, Czechoslovakia, he considered suggestions about the best routes to follow on the forthcoming stages of his journey. Then, in Breslavia, he was joined by another friar, Benedict of Poland.

The brave little band headed farther towards the unknown. They passed through places where memories, tales and frightened faces might well have daunted lesser men.

They travelled through villages and towns that had good cause to remember the Mongols. At Liegnitz, they were reminded vividly of the terrible battle only four years before.

Next they traced their way to Kracovia, the last outpost of Christianity before the mysterious and challenging East. It was here at the Court of the duke Conrad that Giovanni and his companions were fortunate to meet Basil, duke of Vlodomir, a Russian prince who knew the Mongols all too well, having come up against them more than once both in peace and war.

"So you want to go to the Tartars?" he asked. Basil smiled bitterly.

"Then the first point", he said, "and follow it if you want to come back, is to take many presents. The Tartars ask for them obstinately. Heaven help you if they do not get them."

It seemed sensible advice, and Giovanni acquired a large number of beaver skins, before the friars continued their journey, escorted by the duke Basil who was returning to Vlodomir. What was in their minds when there they bade him farewell can be left only to the imagination.

Already their journey had been hard and hazardous, but at least it had been through Christian countries. Every stride forward now was a stride away from safety and their civilisation and a step towards the unknown and the savage. As they rode towards Kiev, they prayed for courage and struggled to forget the sickening sights they saw.

"While we were travelling across this region, we could see innumerable skulls and human bones scattered on the ground."

But reach Kiev they did . . . "a town which used to be rather large and well populated and which now is next to nothing because there remain only 200 houses."

In the meantime, winter had set in and snow covered the endless deserted plain.

What now? Did they wait for the weather to grow more clement or did they press on? Giovanni made his decision when he learned of Mongol horses that "looked for grass hidden under the snow because there is nothing else to eat, as the Tartars have no straw, no hay, no pasture."

On 4th February, 1246, he and his companions bought some of the sturdy, hardy beasts and left Kiev for Kanew on the River Dnieper. There they had to part company with Stephen of Bohemia who suddenly fell ill.

Cruel eyes watched from a distance as the tiny party plodded slowly across desolate no man's land, nearer and nearer to those territories controlled directly by the Mongols.

On the 19th February, the first terrible moment came.

Sunset was near, Giovanni and his few companions were looking for a spot to make camp, when suddenly the ground trembled with the thunder of hoofs. Racing towards them, their bows drawn taut, arrows poised, came a band of Tartars.

"Who are you?" they asked menacingly. "Where are you going?" And it was obvious that one false move or foolish word would have brought a summary end to the expedition.

Giovanni showed at that heart-stopping moment that he did not lack courage. He stared coolly at the vicious shafts.

"We carry important letters to the Court of Kuyuk, the new Great Khan," he replied. That much he had learned at least—the name of the successor to the mighty Genghis. Then he began to hand out food generously.

Without another word, the Mongols turned and galloped away, the breath of their horses panting clouds of white steamy breath into the icy air.

Early next morning the Mongols were back again, but this time they were more high-ranking warriors.

The interrogation was harder and more demanding. Giovanni's further offers of food were disdained curtly. Wanted now was more precise information about the journey of these white men. How dared they cross the frontiers of the Great Khan's territories? Did they know that merciless death would be their only reward for any answer that was unsatisfactory?

Again Giovanni remained calm in the face of their threats. He stared boldly into the penetrating eyes of a Mongol captain and then began to read one of the letters from the Pope.

To his astonishment—and no doubt his everlasting relief—the Mongol nodded, beckoned to his men to relax and granted permission to the tiny band of adventurers to continue their journey. They were also given fresh mounts and guides to escort them to General Corensa, who commanded the border zones from his camp near the River Dnieper.

Riding at a fierce pace from dawn till nightfall, they kept travelling eastwards across stark mountains.

Corensa was a ferocious and capable Mongol general who had doubtless led many of the slaughterous attacks before which Christian Europe had quailed. Before he would even see them, he demanded to see their presents. Basil, duke of Vlodomir, had known his adversaries well, it seemed.

Apparently satisfied with what they offered, Corensa invited Giovanni and Benedict of Poland into his presence. But, before they entered, they were given explicit instructions.

"We were warned to bow three times before his tent, kneeling with the left knee and being careful not to place a foot on the doorway, because whoever does that is punished by death."

Still kneeling, Giovanni explained to Corensa the reason for his mission. He attempted to read the letters, but the interpreter could not translate them, and, at that, Corensa grew bored.

He dismissed the two friars, entrusting them to three Mongol guides, whose orders were to lead them to the Court of Prince Batu along the Volga.

They left on 16th February, "riding for as long as the horses could go. Most days we had fresh horses three or four times, so we were travelling from morning to evening and often at night. But with all that we did not reach Prince Batu until 4th April.

From the Dnieper to the Volga, then, their expedition had taken forty days of hard travelling, during which time Giovanni studied the land through which they were passing, asking the guides for the names of rivers, mountains and tribes.

For the first time they learned the names—indeed the existence—of long rivers like the Dnieper, the Volga, the Don and the Ural. For the first time they gained some idea of the size of the Black Sea. And the names of many of the distant tribes were now known.

Prince Batu—whose court was near the present-day town of Astrakhan—gave them only a cool reception. He asked to see them, read a translation of the letter they were carrying and then allowed them to go on their way, escorted by only two of the Mongol guides given by Corensa.

Through a sprawling countryside, deserted or dotted with small salt lakes, the explorers advanced along a track north of Lake Caspio and Lake Aral until at last, utterly exhausted, they reached the town of Yanghi-kend on the Syr Daria.

From here, on 17th May, they entered nightmare scenery, passing deserted mountains, ruined castles, abandoned villages, skirting sleepy towns, of which they carefully noted the names.

In the town of Omil, in the country of Kitai Neri, they were given brief hospitality in a house belonging to the Emperor himself. And then it was time to start their march again, at last towards the goal for which they longed—towards Karakorum, capital of the Mongol Empire.

Having passed through the valley of the Ili and crossed the pass of Talki, they then saw before them the vast arid stretches of the Gobi Desert, sinister and unfriendly.

But perhaps Karakorum was not far beyond it. Only that thought kept Giovanni and his friends going.

"We travelled very quickly, because the Tartars accompanying us had orders to take us as speedily as possible to the solemn Court of the Emperor. We therefore rose early in the mornings and travelled often until night without eating.

At long, long last their monumental ride reached its end. The travellers had passed along the route the Chinese call "the northern way of the Celestial Mountains." From their camp at night, they could see the lights of Karakorum.

Having left Yanghi-kend on 17th May they had travelled for 67 days, covering the incredible distance of about 2,500 miles.

Now Giovanni had to await the summons of the Great Khan—Emperor of those Tartar hordes whose very names were dreaded by men, women and children everywhere.

At last the proud and mighty Mongol Emperor allowed the Pope's ambassadors into his presence.

Kuyuk Khan did not at once receive the two friars from the West, but he had been kept carefully informed of their progress. Understandably he was curious to hear what they had to tell him. But he knew already what the Pope had written.

For a while he gave Giovanni and the others lodging where they could rest and recover from the ardours of their epic journey.

The splendour of the Court, its grandeur and the military power evident everywhere made a tremendous impact on Giovanni. In his report, he carefully described what he had seen, especially the customs and the costumes of the Mongols.

It was the cold Autumn before Kuyuk agreed to grant an audience and listen to the message of the papal envoys. His face remained inscrutable as he listened to the sorrowful words of the Pope.

"Wishing that all may live lovingly united under the fear of God, we warn all of you . . . and we pray you and urge you strongly to immediately stop such warlike actions, especially against Christians."

Having listened to the message, Kuyuk said he would prepare and answer and then dismissed the ambassadors. A few days later Giovanni was given a letter to deliver to the Pope.

"Oh Pope," it read, "if you want peace and friendship with us, you will come to us with all your kings and dignitaries to hear our answer and our will. And you will give to us your subservience and your tributes.

"And if you will not listen to our advice and will not come, we will assume that you want to make war upon us. After that, we cannot say what will happen. Only God knows."

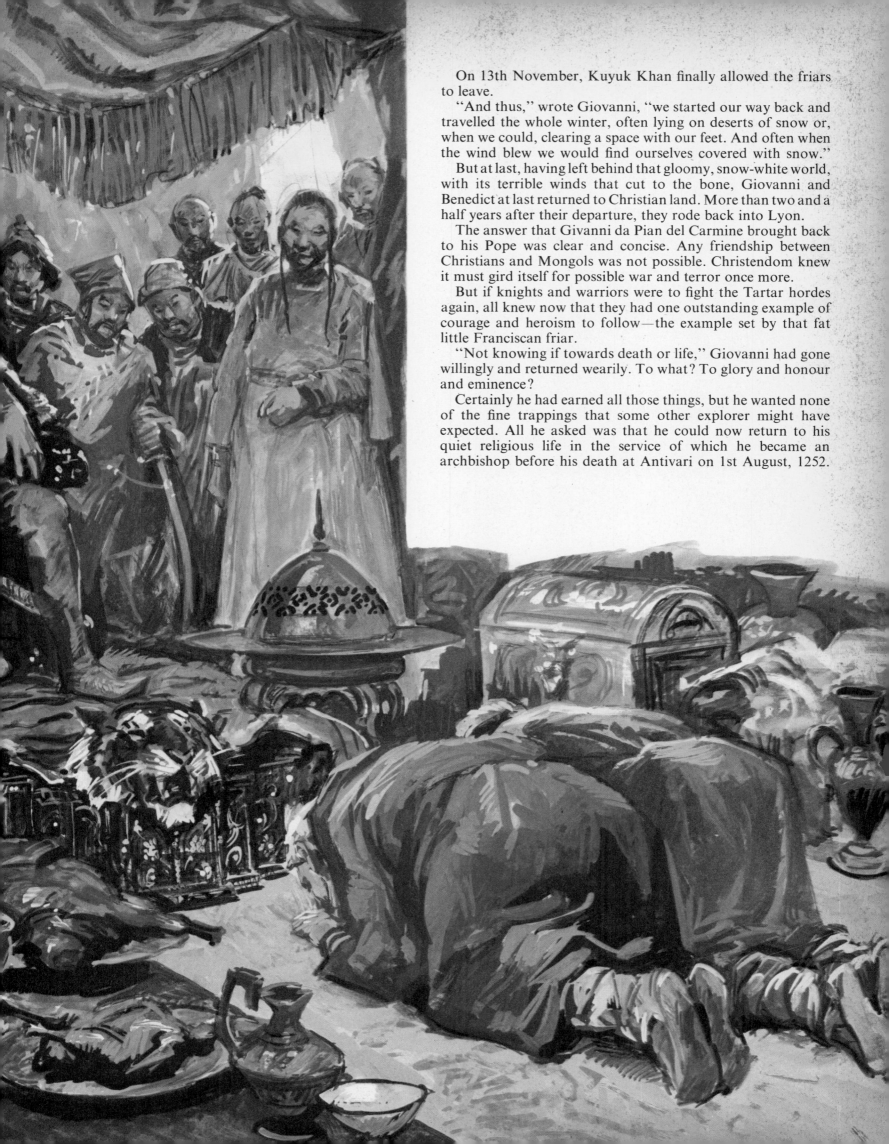

On 13th November, Kuyuk Khan finally allowed the friars to leave.

"And thus," wrote Giovanni, "we started our way back and travelled the whole winter, often lying on deserts of snow or, when we could, clearing a space with our feet. And often when the wind blew we would find ourselves covered with snow."

But at last, having left behind that gloomy, snow-white world, with its terrible winds that cut to the bone, Giovanni and Benedict at last returned to Christian land. More than two and a half years after their departure, they rode back into Lyon.

The answer that Givanni da Pian del Carmine brought back to his Pope was clear and concise. Any friendship between Christians and Mongols was not possible. Christendom knew it must gird itself for possible war and terror once more.

But if knights and warriors were to fight the Tartar hordes again, all knew now that they had one outstanding example of courage and heroism to follow—the example set by that fat little Franciscan friar.

"Not knowing if towards death or life," Giovanni had gone willingly and returned wearily. To what? To glory and honour and eminence?

Certainly he had earned all those things, but he wanted none of the fine trappings that some other explorer might have expected. All he asked was that he could now return to his quiet religious life in the service of which he became an archbishop before his death at Antivari on 1st August, 1252.

ROBERT E. PEARY

It was a terrible time to be at sea in those cruel, churning Arctic waters. Winds howled through the rigging, icy blasts battered and tossed the ship like a piece of abandoned flotsam and the crew lurched crazily backwards, forwards and sideways as sheets of black, freezing water lashed the decks.

Every muscle bulging with effort, Robert Peary struggled to hold the wheel, strained like a grizzly bear to stop it spinning from control. His face, rimed white with caked frost, contorted at every roll and rise of the creaking *Kite* and yet his eyes burned like glowing coals as he stared back defiantly at the raging elements around him.

"Iceberg!" He barely heard the warning cry amid the screaming, wailing winds. But seconds later he recoiled momentarily as its huge bulk loomed from the darkness and bore down on the ship slowly, in no hurry to strike its stunning blow.

The *Kite* was brushed aside effortlessly—though fortunately not shattered into a thousand splinters as other ships before— and now a scream of pain was scything through the storm.

Horror, crystallised on each face, held everyone rooted to the spot. Whirling round wildly, like an upended carousel out of control, was the ship's wheel. Trapped between two of its spokes was one of Peary's legs.

Even as his companions rushed towards him, he made a superhuman effort to disentangle himself and lay there groaning. A swift glance revealed to them the dismaying news. Their leader's leg was fractured all the way up to the hip.

And this before they had even sighted Greenland, their destination, let alone reached it to begin its exploration, the mission with which they had been charged by the Science Academy of Philadelphia in 1891.

Robert Edwin Peary himself put an end to their despair. "Get this ship back on course," he told them in pain-filled gasps. "Get us to Greenland, and then we can set out to do what we came here for. Forget my leg. We'll have that fixed somehow or other."

His men looked at him uneasily. Could they now possibly even contemplate a journey through the snows and ices of the great North? The determination in Peary's voice said they could. And so they did.

Reaching their base at Smith Bay, they strapped their leader to a board and hauled him about his duties on a sledge.

Sooner than anyone thought possible, Peary was limping about, forcing himself along on long testing walks across the rough and frozen land, determined to start that trek.

With Peary were his wife, Jo, the first white woman to venture into Greenland, Dr. Frederick Cook—of whom we shall hear later—and Matthew Henson, Peary's faithful black servant, who was to be his inseparable companion in many epic assaults on those polar territories.

"I am ready," growled Peary one April day in 1892, and with a few companions he left for the interior, sledging onwards at a hard and unrelenting pace.

On that particular expedition he reached a grim, forbidding mountain at latitude 81° 37′ North and decided that this was the farthest-point of Greenland. It was a mistake, as it turned out—but he meanwhile established that Greenland was an island, second only to Australia in size, and also discovered Independence Bay.

Americans everywhere were proud of that achievement, buoyant that one of their countrymen had shown the same pioneering spirit that had largely won their own continent.

'This time, Mr. President,
to the Pole or to Hell,'
said Robert Peary.
And so began the last of
the Arctic hero's many treks . . .

AN AMERICAN VETERAN ON TOP OF THE WORLD

In February, 1908, the Roosevelt nosed its way into Cape Columbia. The do-or-die bid for the Pole was about to start.

L. ARCAS-70

For Robert Peary, though, it was merely one stepping stone in a polar career that he meant to be long and glorious. No sooner was he returned from Greenland, than his mind was aflame with more blazing ambitions—and blazing more fiercely than any of them was one in particular: to be the first man ever to stand upon the snowy axis of the world.

That ambition, that tremendous obsession, had been within him for a long time.

Born in Cresson, Pennsylvania on 6th May, 1856, he was apparently a lonely child, given to fits of depression, with an embarrassing lisp that took him years of effort to rid. His choice of career did not suggest he was attracted to the icy wastes on the roof of the world. He decided to study civil engineering, and entered the United States Navy.

Possibly the most romantic suggestion of all as to why he should one day set his sights North was that the tropical suffocating stuffiness of Nicaragua—where in 1885 he surveyed the route of a canal from the Atlantic to the Pacific—made him long for chillier ventures. What, in fact, he probably did find in that humid corner of the world was a real purpose to his life. He must have realised then that he had reached an age where he wanted to dedicate himself to something worthwhile—and the frozen North seemed to offer the greatest challenge.

Peary was thirty when he first landed on the coast of Greenland and fixed his stern, appraising eyes on its mysterious black cliffs, gigantic glaciers that overhung the sea and the eternal white canopy of frozen snow and ice.

Starting from the Bay of Disko with a Danish companion named Maigaard, Peary began his first trek inland, covering a distance of about 100 miles and reaching a height of 7,500 feet.

Not an outstanding start to polar conquest, but Peary had expected no phenomenal outcome from that initial journey. All he wanted was to learn things, and to measure his own resistance to cold, hunger and tiredness.

And he knew on his return that he could one day bid for the greatest goal. He had learned enough about himself to accept the challenge of the farthest North.

But probably most important of all on that first minor trip was that he worked out a new concept of Arctic exploration. He realised that a small party of skilled explorers could use the assistance of Eskimos during their travels.

Five years later Peary returned to Greenland on that voyage aboard the *Kite*, when his leg was shattered—and there his courage and stamina was proved to the hilt.

He returned in 1893, 1894, 1896 and again in 1897. Each trek he made was longer and more audacious than the last. Every moment he spent in the North, he learnt something. He learnt what it was like to be buried in the deep snow, and how it felt to disappear beneath cracking ice. And all the time he was building lasting friendships with the Eskimos.

From them he learned how to build igloos, how to speak their language fluently, and indeed almost became one of them. They were ordinary people, he felt, and yet they could resist the cold, hunger and the biting winds better than any other people on Earth. If he was one day to reach the North Pole, ought he not try to imitate them as best he could? Should he not dress, eat, drink and speak like them?

All this he did and the Eskimos loved him for it. His affection for them, too, was great, but it in no way diminished his burning desire soon to stand on top of the world.

By 1898 he was ready to try.

But the Arctic does not treat its challengers lightly. Peary made several forays into the wilds to reconnoitre the most suitable routes for his grand bid, and on one trek he suddenly started to feel awful pains in his feet.

Stranded in a lonely, wind-blasted ice-house, miles from even the crudest civilised community, his heart began to sink as the dread realisation set in. Both his feet were frozen.

Robert Edwin Peary knew his North too well to turn his face from the stupefying truth of what must happen next. If gangrene were not to eat his feet away, he had to lose his toes.

Shaking, sick with a temperature, strained by anguish, he nevertheless refused to surrender to despair.

His feet covered by the warm skin of a musk-ox, Peary was finally rushed back to his ship and hurried to the doctor of the expedition. Carefully he examined Peary's feet before murmuring reassuringly, "We'll see what we can do."

Peary answered firmly. "No, do it now."

At once the amputation began. There was no alternative. When he came round, Peary had lost nine toes. Many men might have given up at this point—but not Peary. Call him dauntless, defiant or downright stubborn, call him what you will, but within a few weeks he was on his broken feet again, staggering lamely along on further marches.

"When my leave is finished, or when I have reached the Pole, I will be ready to go back." That was all he said when his companions questioned the wisdom of his actions.

He pushed forward again in the spring and summer of 1900 as far as 82° 39′ North. Two years later—with his faithful servant Henson and a few Eskimos—he tried again.

It was a terrible journey, punctuated by storms that seemed to shake the very world apart, and forced up insurmountable walls of ice. Having reached 84° 17′, Peary had to give up.

In his diary he wrote, "The game is lost. My dream is finished. I did my best, but it has been a fight harder than any other. I cannot do the impossible."

He returned to America exhausted and disappointed. But he was far from tamed. At the back of his mind was the thought that he had failed only because of his damaged feet. He underwent an operation in Philadelphia, and soon made preparations to fling his last challenge at the North.

Peary had few illusions left. "I was 53, an age beyond which," he was to write later, "no man would think of going to the Pole. I was in a period of physical decline. Maybe I had already passed the age at which people retire from the fight and leave their place to the young."

But if he now lacked youth, he still had enormous experience. Furthermore, he felt convinced that defeat or tragedy were reserved only for the incautious.

He had studied his route down to every last detail, preparing a plan of campaign in which advance parties would leave supplies along the line of march, so that Peary himself could make the last decisive bid for the Pole itself.

In 1905, a ship had been built to Peary's design, specially constructed to cope with the crushing pressures of pack ice. He had named it the *Roosevelt*, in honour of the then new president of the United States.

As it left to take its dogged hero towards his final attempt on the Pole, President Roosevelt himself was there to wish Peary luck.

Peary considered it important to build lasting friendships with the Eskimos. From them he learned how to build igloos.

But they kept going, spurred on by the passionate aim and will of their grizzled leader until, on 29th March, they reached 87° 46′ North, after travelling 280 snow-blasted miles.

Everyone clustered around the hardened old American. This was it. This was where they parted company at the last base before the Pole. Well-wishing smiles of encouragement, the final good-luck waves, and the main party turned back, their dogs hauling away their sledges to the distant, blurred horizon.

Peary, his faithful Matt Henson and four Eskimos—Okeah, Eginguah, Ootah and Scelgoo—were left alone with 40 dogs and 5 sledges. Beyond them was the elusive Pole, which they planned to reach in five marches of 25 miles each.

On the 1st April, the dash for the Pole was on.

Every yard forward they went, Peary's exhilaration mounted.

35° below zero, and their trek was growing harder.

"I believe in your success, Peary," he said, "if this is possible to a man."

"Thank you," replied the crusty old veteran of the North. "This time, Mr. President, to the Pole or to Hell."

Peary's Eskimos greeted him with delight when the *Roosevelt* nosed into its anchorage at Cape Columbia in February, 1908. They paddled their kayaks joyfully around the ship. "You are like the sun," they cried. "You always come back!"

Departure day for the do-or-die Polar bid, Peary decided, was to be 28th February, 1909.

That day, the trail-breaking and supply-laying parties set off across the ice, followed by supporting groups, and Peary's own tiny band. 24 men, 133 dogs and 19 sledges—divided into groups of three men each—strung out across the white wilderness.

Everything seemed to be conspiring against them at first. Howling winds threw razor-sharp particles of ice and jagged fragments of hard snow against the men's faces until they were covered in frozen blood.

In many places, the rough ice was broken by channels of freezing water which had to be by-passed or crossed only at the greatest risk and with the most alarming difficulty.

And how could anyone describe the cold that seemed to peel the skin and soul from a man? At one point, a bottle of brandy in Peary's furs froze solid at a temperature of 50° below zero.

The marches were going well, his luck was holding and so was the weather. Sometimes he would climb on to a spur of ice and look Northwards, trying to imagine what the Pole would be like.

The final march was completed at 10 a.m. on 6th April, when Peary made camp and took an observation of the noonday sun. His latitude was 89 degrees, 57 minutes, 11 seconds North. He was a mere three miles from the Pole.

"We are going to stop here," he called to the others. "We need some sleep and to get back some of our strength." Then quietly he walked into his small tent.

But it was a restless sleep. He kept waking up in a frenzy of excitement. Wide awake, he took his diary and wrote in a trembling hand: "The Pole, at last. The cost of three centuries. My dream and my aim for 20 years. Mine at last. I cannot believe it."

Early next day they swept forward, almost running the whole way, driving on the dogs faster and faster. And then Peary raised his hand to halt. Out came the instruments, he peered at them closely and in a surge of emotion realised his excitement had driven him past his goal.

It was done. The North Pole was won!

But, to make perfectly certain, he set the seal on his triumph by sledging a criss-cross northwards course, taking a series of sun-sights.

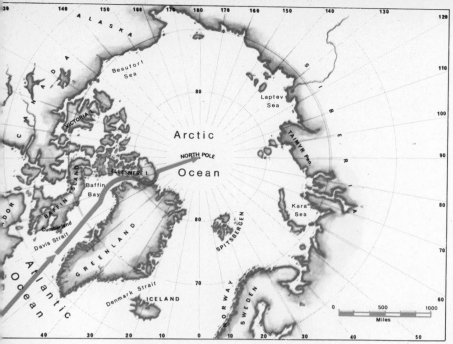

and despair for the rugged, never-give-in Peary. Awaiting him was the cruellest blow.

On his return to civilisation, he was greeted by the news that his former friend—Dr. Frederick Cook, companion on that earlier voyage to Greenland when Peary had shattered his leg—claimed he himself had reached the Pole the previous year.

Peary reacted terribly. The fury of his words was more biting than any blizzard that had blown countless fragments of jagged ice into his face.

"Liar! Liar! Liar!" he thundered—and his outspoken accusations rebounded on him, leaving *him* accused of the very treachery and deceit with which he had branded Cook.

The controversy continued until 1911 when Cook's claims were at last rejected, and later evidence of other fraudulent claims of his left doubt in no one's mind that Peary was the true conqueror of the Pole.

As someone said, "Cook was a liar and a gentleman. Peary was neither." But, at least, his rightful awards and honours were showered upon him before his death in 1920. A great and courageous man received the glory and recognition he deserved.

Finally certain he was on top of the globe, the American explorer ordered the final stop and planted five flags in the ice—the American one which his wife had given him 15 years earlier; the flag of his college; the red, white and blue of world freedom and peace; that of the American Naval League and finally the Red Cross.

Peary shook hands with Henson and the Eskimos. Though the Eskimos could not quite understand the delight and emotion of their leader, they smiled happily at his satisfaction. Their friend had come from far away and reached where he wanted to arrive. He had won. They could understand this.

Not a thing troubled their return to base. It took them only sixteen days to make their way back, and as they came over the fringe that separated the ice from dry land, everyone erupted in wild cheers of delight at the sight of the raised hands signifying victory. "They jumped, shouted and sang until they dropped."

But brewing in the near future was shock, disappointment

At last they stood in triumph at the North Pole. Peary's twenty-year old dream was finally realised.

DAVID LIVINGSTONE

THE FATHER OF AFRICA

Little David Livingstone peered over the edge of the bed coverlet and stared with big eyes at the pale old man who lay there, the flickering candlelight casting moving shadows on his sunken face and white hair.

Gathered round the bed were others—men, women and children —some of them dabbing furtively at weeping eyes as the old man found it an effort even to breathe in the big, gloomy room. His eyes opened wearily, then feebly he beckoned them all closer, starting to talk, his every word laboured.

"All my life," he said in a burring Scottish accent, "I have looked with the greatest care into the traditions of our family, and I have never found among us a dishonest man. I have no wealth or possessions to hand among you, but I do leave you this most valuable advice. Be honest."

His words delivered so sincerely, the great-grandfather of David Livingstone breathed his last. The young child was led from the room, holding his father's hand, thinking about that last moving saying of the old man on whose frail knees he had sometimes bounced and laughed.

They were words, often repeated to him by his father, that he never forgot. Printed forever in his mind and heart, they were to influence his life totally, granting him a philosophy that helped him tread a path to greatness.

Just over sixty years had passed since the bloodstained battle of Culloden had helped bring an already impoverished Scotland further to her knees when David came into the world. Born in Blantyre, Scotland, on 19th March, 1813, he was one of tens of thousands born into the dire poverty that the early 19th century offered most Scottish people.

At the age of ten, he was sent out to work for a pitiful wage in a spinning-mill. But somehow, because his parents had encouraged him in any leisure time they had and he had listened carefully during the little while he had spent at school, he knew how to read and write.

He even took his books to the mill, putting them on the loom, so that he could read them while he was working, something about which the other workers often complained.

By the time he was 19, David had learned Latin, had a fair grasp of Greek, and was also studying botany, anatomy and the natural sciences. There were other books, too, that fascinated him—tales written by travellers, the exciting accounts of explorers and the moving memoirs of missionaries in far away countries.

The boy was growing into the man, and in his mind was growing the idea that his destiny lay not in a mill, but in the service of other people whom he might help and educate. More than anything, he decided, he wanted to become a missionary.

China fascinated him most. He knew there were millions of poor and starving people there, and he wanted to help them. Leaving the mill, making many personal sacrifices, he went to study theology and medicine at the Anderson College in Glasgow before applying to the Missionary Society in London to be sent to China.

All was ready for his departure in 1840 when suddenly he was forced to cancel all his plans. What was to become known as the 'Opium War' had broken out between Britain and China. It was quite impossible to send any more missionaries out there.

But there was a mission in South Africa, David was told, if he wished to accept it. He did, though only reluctantly. For some reason, Africa held for him none of the same mystery and challenge of China.

David Livingstone arrived in Cape Town in 1841, travelled from there to Algoa Bay, and then went on to the Kuruman Mission in Bechuanaland where he began his work.

For eight years he devoted himself to his task. He was continuously on the move, reaching undiscovered villages where he would cure the sick, offer advice to anyone who needed it, help the natives build their huts and, at the same time, preach the word of God to them in simple stories.

Continuously moving around the country, Livingstone visited undiscovered villages and helped to cure the sick.

As he learned to understand the natives, he came to respect them and their way of life. He made a point of learning their various dialects, and he gathered from them how best he could travel and survive in the seemingly boundless continent. A real and lasting love for Africa started to grow within him.

Slowly but surely, David came to know his adopted land. He also knew its dangers. In 1844, he was clawed badly by a lion and escaped with his life only by the sheerest good fortune.

As it was, that encounter turned out to be a turning point in his life. His wounds were treated at Kuruman by the head of the Mission, the Reverend Moffat, an Irishman for whom David had the highest regard and affection. But even greater affection he had for Moffat's daughter, Mary. David fell very much in love with her, and married her that same year, 1844.

With a young wife to support now, and the possibility of children sometime in the future, it might have been thought that David would ask for a quieter mission. But nothing of the sort. Instead, the couple searched for wider horizons, travelling the country in an old cart towed by oxen. David had found the ideal companion for the kind of life he wished to live.

Sometimes their travels would take them to the boundaries of the great Kalahari Desert, and as he looked down on it from the mountains, David often would ask himself what lay beyond that far-stretching plain of burning sands.

Actually he had been told the answer often enough. There was nothing but more sand and more mountains. The centre of Africa was scorched and parched by the sun at its hottest. The great continent was arid desert, merciless to any living thing.

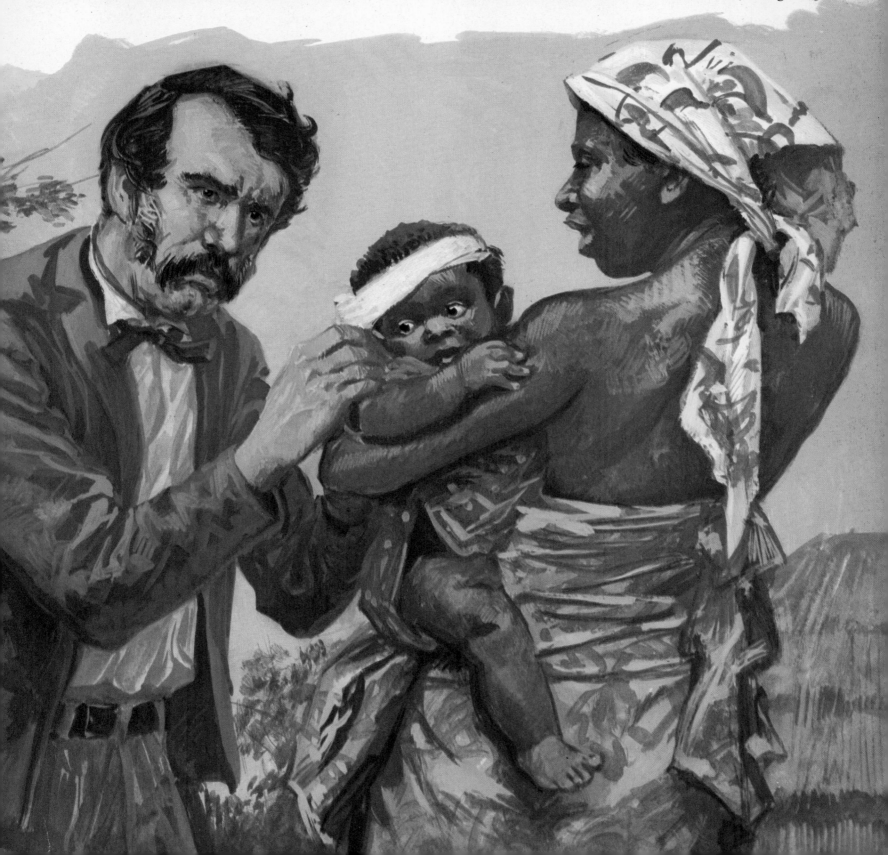

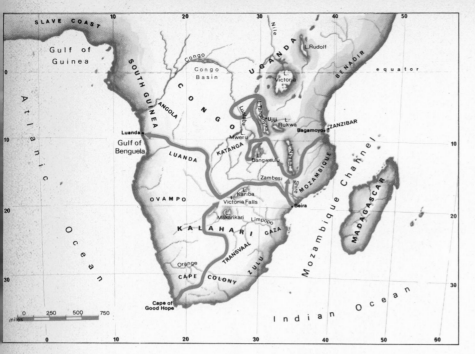

At least, that was the opinion of scientists back home in every part of Europe. They hadn't actually visited the place to find out for themselves, but everything they had studied led them to their conclusion, and David had no reason to dispute it, until he recalled a conversation with a native who said that beyond the Kalahari lay green lands, sprawling forests, long, winding rivers and a great lake. The man even knew the name of the lake, which was called Ngami.

David's mind wrestled with doubts. Surely these poor blacks could not know better than eminent scientists? On the other hand, though, why not? After all, Africa was still an unread book.

He began to smile to himself. What if those fertile lands did exist beyond the Kalahari? How he would love to see the expressions on the faces of those 'book explorers' back home. And what a tremendous opportunity it would offer to men like himself who wanted to help and educate the Africans.

His thoughts were still on the matter when he met another native who talked about Lake Ngami. But this man revealed even more. In particular, he talked about the kingdom of Sebituane, chief of the Makalolo tribe, who lived north of the great lake.

Now David was convinced. His excitement mounted. He wanted to know, see and learn more. Until that point in his life, he had been first and foremost a missionary. But now another spirit clasped him more strongly—the spirit of the explorer.

Within a short time, he was making plans for a journey to those green lands far away.

Quite by chance, he was fortunate enough at the time to meet two British hunters, Mungo Murray and William Oswell, who were also set on heading northwards across and beyond the Kalahari. They asked him if he would accompany them as their guide and interpreter.

In June, 1849, the expedition set out from Kolobeng on a trek that was to be slow and tiring, but utterly fascinating. With forty pairs of oxen hauling four laden carts, they made their way across vast expanses of untouched sands or sometimes along ancient caravan routes, long since abandoned.

Throughout the journey David took notes of everything he saw, stopping every now and again to calculate their position and height above sea level.

Most surprising of all to him, however, was that the Kalahari was not that awful place of death that everyone had predicted. Here and there, they found water holes and there were traces of human habitation. More than once, in fact, they were attacked by mysterious tribes who rained arrows on them and tried to steal their oxen.

Finally the Kalahari was crossed, and now they awaited the answer to their question about what lay beyond. On 1st August, they found out. That day they stood overlooking the fabulous Lake Ngami, shimmering in the sun before them. The natives had been right all along.

Now standing there were the first men ever to set eyes on the lake, a fact that delighted Oswell and Murray. But David Livingstone was strangely silent as his eyes wandered not over the lake's rippling waters but towards the land beyond.

"What is down there?", he asked. And in that question a new ambition was born.

The party made its way back to Kolobeng in due course, but while they travelled David was already making plans for a new expedition.

Next time, he decided, he intended to make his way directly to King Sebituane, taking with him this time his wife and the three small children they now had.

Their first attempt was a failure. Though they crossed the Kalahari, when they reached Lake Ngami, they all caught malaria which laid them low. To make things worse, many of the natives were talking of a terrible fly, which they called the tsetse. Further north, it was said to be spreading a disease that was slaughtering men and animals indiscriminately. Reluctantly, bitterly disappointed, the Livingstones turned back.

But, in 1851, they were on their way again, on a dramatic journey that filled David with a new sense of wonder. Finally they reached Linjianti, the village of Sebituane, where David made a silent prayer that all would be well.

To his delight, he was welcomed warmly by the black king, and there grew almost immediately a strong and loyal friendship between the two. David's cup of happiness seemed overflowing. This was why he was in Africa—to help build a new age of brotherhood between blacks and whites. The ideal seemed more than a fanciful possibility when Sebituane gave his permission for David to build a new mission in his kingdom.

Almost without warning, tragedy came, upsetting the Scottish missionary and explorer deeply.

Sadly, Sebituane had a serious infection of the lungs and died within a few days, despite David's desperate efforts to cure him. At once, the missionary feared that this would be the end of everything, for the Makalolos were superstitious and might think he had brought them death and bad luck. But nothing of the sort. Now led by Sebituane's nephew, Sekeletu, they did not change their attitude towards him at all.

Now David Livingstone felt he had found the door through which he could enter the obscure heart of Africa.

It seemed, too, that he might have found the actual route into the interior. The Makalolos told him about a great river that flowed north, a huge rushing, tumbling torrent the natives called Zambesi—the 'Great Flow'—and at once David asked to see it.

Given bearers, supplies and guides, he set out in search of it, and in June, 1851, he stood staring across at its far bank, at least 2,000 feet across.

He gazed in awe at the most magnificent falls he had ever seen—the Victoria Falls, as he named them in honour of his queen.

As more of his native bearers fled in fear of the slave-traders, David's journey grew harder and the forests more difficult to hack a way through.

Confronted by such mighty splendour and magnificence, David now found hundreds of further questions pouring through his mind. Where did the Zambesi start? Where did it go? Into the Indian Ocean? Or did it marry up with the Congo or the Nile? And then those other questions about the north still remained to be answered. He could see more mountains in the distance. What lay beyond them?

But as often happens when a man sets his eyes on a goal, something comes along to mar the sense of excitement and anticipation he experiences. So it proved with David Livingstone as he stood on the threshold of further great discoveries.

To his grief and horror he noticed during his stay with the Makalolos that the trading of slaves flourished. In exchange for firearms or whatever goods they needed, they sold prisoners from other tribes into slavery. In fact, they often waged wars with other tribes just so they could take prisoners for these transactions in human flesh.

He said nothing to his hosts, but already grown within him was a profound loathing for such inhuman bartering, and he planned to do whatever he could to suppress slavery. As he headed back south, he was forming plans to inform the world

that the slave trade was still rampant in Africa, and he meant to find ways of fighting and destroying it.

Military action was out of the question, he believed. More effective by far would be a commerical 'war'. In David's opinion the slave trade was what it was—a 'trade'—because there were no other goods to exchange.

If he could encourage the opening and building of roads and commercial routes through Africa, real trade between the coast and the interior would become possible and the marketing of men bound to cease.

Word of his new hopes and aims reached the ears of the Boers, and at this time they became more threatening—so much so that in 1852 David decided to send Mary and the children to England. He journeyed there with them to find a home, but set out almost immediately for Africa again. This time he was absorbed in a new and ambitious project—to identify and chart the course of the Zambesi.

His reception when he returned was distinctly hostile. The Boers now mocked him as an interferer and meddler in things that did not concern him. Missionaries were meant to preach, their bible teachings, they said, nothing else.

To intimidate David Livingstone and drive him away from Africa forever, they attacked the mission at Kolobeng, killed many of the people there, destroyed all the medical supplies and burnt all his books.

Gentle, honest and kind the Scottish missionary might have been, but there is nothing like a Scotsman aroused. Fury welled up inside David and his determination hardened.

"I wanted to open the heart of Africa to Christianity, to commerce, to freedom and civilisation," he wrote. The Boers wanted to obstruct the passage to teachers and traders through the country they thought they could exploit with slavery. But if Boers wanted to close Africa to the Europeans," he concluded "I was absolutely decided to open it up."

He left again, alone. In autumn, 1853, he met up again with Sekeletu at Scesceke on the Zambesi, and accompanied by 27 natives, he started the first of his great journeys.

He meant to trace back the course of the river, searching, as he said, for somewhere suitable to set up a mission. Really, though, he wanted to study the course to see if it was at all navigable. What if the Zambesi turned out to be a great commercial route which could strike a deadly blow against slavery?

It was a terrible journey, plagued by hardships, through unknown regions. More than once David despaired of success. More than once his faithful Makalolos asked him to turn back, but he would not give up.

In many past expeditions, and even more in future ones, guns were of the greatest importance in opening the way. But Livingstone never shot anyone. Even when his life was at stake and he had to draw a gun, he merely levelled it at whoever was threatening him, but he never pressed the trigger. The magnetic force of his eyes always seemed to grant him victory.

Victory for his expedition came in April, 1854, when Livingstone and his men reached Cassange, a Portuguese outpost near the mountains of present-day Angola, near where they found the upper reaches of the Zambesi. From Cassange the expedition had little trouble reaching Luanda, on the Atlantic coast.

We can imagine the scene that 31st May, 1854, as their party emerged from the jungles and stumbled towards the ramshackle port of Luanda on the western ocean. Soon the news was sweeping the town that for the first time a man had left the centre of Africa and reached the coast.

The Portuguese were stupefied. Several British traders and travellers went wild with excitement. Livingstone, thin and tired, his eyes still bright with fever, was chaired through the streets on their shoulders.

Many of the British in Luanda wanted to be with David on his return to Britain to describe his great adventure. All of them were amazed when he announced that he did not intend to return yet. He admitted honestly that he would like to go back to London to see his family and talk of his journey, but first he had a promise to honour.

With him were his faithful Makalolos, and he had promised to take them back home. So it was that he turned his back on the ocean and headed once more into the interior, making for the Zambesi, along which they retraced their course. Many months later, they were welcomed back with surprise and joy by Sekeletu and his people, who had long since believed them lost and dead.

David was deep in thought again even as their return was celebrated. He knew now that the Zambesi could not be opened as a commercial waterway, at least in its western reaches. But what about its eastern course? Perhaps trade could enter the heart of Africa that way? That was the next question to which he would seek an answer.

In November, 1855—with a hundred men whom Sekeletu had gladly put at his disposal—he set out along the opposite course of the Zambesi.

As early as the 14th of that month, he gathered that the Zambesi might not make the trade route he so badly wanted to find. On that day, there tumbled before his eyes the mighty, rushing waters of one of the most magnificent waterfalls in the world—the enormous Victoria Falls, so named that day by Livingstone in honour of his queen. Their beauty was breathtaking, but they ruled out the possibility of navigating the Zambesi, he felt.

Still David pressed on, until March, 1856, when he reached Quelimane, on the Indian Ocean, another Portuguese colony at the delta of the Zambesi.

One of the most splendid journeys in the history of exploration had been accomplished. A man had actually crossed the whole African continent from west to east.

What David wanted now was rest, and he returned at once to his homeland where he was welcomed like the conqueror he was. Honours in plenty were heaped on him. He was the greatest hero of his day, possibly the most famous man in Britain at the time. Scientists and geographers clamoured for his attention, and listened eagerly and attentively to the lectures he gave. His book *Missionary Travels and Researches in South Africa* was read avidly.

Possibly the only people who viewed him unfavourably were members of the Missionary Society in London. In a cool, acidly polite letter, they reproached him for dedicating himself to exploration rather than to missionary work.

Whatever his feelings about their condemnation of his activities, his urge to continue exploring the vast continent did not die. In March, 1858, he left London once more for Africa, this time at the head of an expedition sponsored by the British Government. Its purpose was to make a general study of Central Africa, positively identifying the course of the Zambesi, making observations about the country's physical characteristics, its vegetation and wildlife, and establishing friendly relations with the people there so that trade might be encouraged in the future.

Aboard a small steamboat, the *Ma-Robert*, the expedition sailed from the delta of the Zambesi and along its course, only to discover what Livingstone already suspected, that the great river was not completely navigable.

The geographical discoveries of that journey were the most important things to emerge. Livingstone discovered Lake Shiriva, and then, on 16th September, 1859, following vague directions from the natives, he reached the shores of a lake that seemed to stretch out as far as the eye could see, like some sprawling inland sea among a forested and hilly land.

He had stumbled upon Lake Nyasa, and determined to explore it fully he spent all his personal savings to buy a sturdy steamboat which he named the *Lady Nyasa*. Aboard it he started a systematic identification of the enormous lake.

Unfortunately, feelings among members of the expedition were not the most comradely. David could not exert the same leadership over his party as he could over his natives, and several bitter quarrels arose, in particular with his brother Charles who was with the expedition. Everyone differed in the aims he wanted to achieve, half the party at least were set on building up commercial and political interests, matters that didn't interest David in the slightest.

News of the misunderstandings and quarrels filtered back to Britain, and the fact that very little commercial success seemed to have been achieved led to the Government informing Livingstone that his official position as British Consul for the East Coast of Africa was to be ended at the end of 1863 and their sponsorship of his mission withdrawn.

It was a bitter blow, though less bitter than the one he received in the early months of 1862. Sailing down the Zambesi to meet his wife Mary who had come to be reunited with him in Africa, he was greeted with the terrible news that she had died suddenly of tropical fever.

Cruelly hurt by the whole turn of events, he returned to London in April, 1864, welcomed this time by no cheering crowds nor showered with any honours, even though he had made important new geographical discoveries. Some people even blamed him for the massacre of a party of missionaries who had followed in his footsteps to Lake Nyasa and had been shot by marauding slave merchants.

For over a year David nursed the wounds inflicted on his spirit by these setbacks. He remained quietly at the home of his brother Charles, writing another book and attempting to interest public opinion in the suppression of the slave trade which still flourished.

But in the back of his mind were plans for yet another expedition to Africa. By the time he was ready to leave in January, 1866, he had won back the sympathy of the Royal Geographical Society and certain members of the Government, who gave their blessing—and funds—to help him. This time his intention was to clarify once and for all the mysteries of the Nile, the Congo and the Zambesi.

For six years this expedition pushed itself on one of the cruellest, most heartbreaking and perilous journeys ever.

Leaving the coast slightly north of Cape Delgado, David began his journey inland towards Lake Nyasa, making a dangerous and exhausting march through unexplored territory until finally he saw the shores of the lake before him once more.

This time it was one of the most horrifying sights he had ever seen. Whole villages had been destroyed, the fields were pillaged and the natives had disappeared. Everywhere there were signs that the slave-dealers had been plying their inhuman trade.

Then, as it proved impossible to build a boat to cross the lake, the expedition had to walk a distance of nearly 500 miles, during which most of the porters quit, scared by the threat of the slave dealers.

Most unfortunate of all, while fleeing, one of the porters took with him the whole stock of medicines. Soon afterwards David was struck down by malaria and had not a grain of quinine with which to dose himself.

Accompanied by Henry Morton Stanley, he sailed around Lake Tanganyika, sketching an accurate map of the great inland sea.

Yet somehow he drew on hidden reserves and kept going. Trembling with fever, he forced his emaciated body onwards through land that seemed ready to swallow them forever.

At last he reached Lake Meru and there he saw the waters of a river, the Luapula, which flowed towards the Congo.

"Where does that river come from?" he asked. Some natives pointed south. "There is a lake. The Bengueolo. The river comes from there."

Livingstone started his march again, but so bad was his health that he almost died, saved only at the last moment by a slave merchant—a bitter irony of fate.

David identified the Bengueolo, but he knew he could not go on much farther. He ordered what few men who still remained to make for Ujiji on Lake Tanganyika, where they arrived in February, 1869.

His hopes that they might find supplies there were cruelly dashed. Everything that had arrived for him from the coast had been stolen. Again he had only his strong spirit on which to lean for survival.

Incredibly he set out again, this time north-west, reaching the River Lualaba and spending a year in that region trying to learn something about it—without success.

On and on Livingstone kept travelling—as always, taking notes about everything. All too often he was witness to the cruel massacres of the slave dealers. By this time the slave trade was at its peak. Never before had David Livingstone felt so weak and lost.

Still he sought information about the Lualaba, which he thought might be the upper course of the White Nile.

"Yes, bwana," a native told him, "the river goes towards the place where the sun sets and at the same time north, It crosses the country where the copper is."

"What is the name of this country?"

"They call it Katanga."

Although he could hardly stand, despite fever and the scabs and ulcers that covered him, Livingstone wanted to go on. He tried to find a boat in which to go downstream and explore the river, but could not find one. Only then did he give up, and resign himself to returning to Ujiji.

The trek back proved dreadfully painful for him. He was able to make it only in short stages, with many long rests during which he was forced to try to regain a little strength. Only in mid-October, 1871, did he reach the village. And, once there, he settled down to await his death, which he knew could not be far off.

As the world knows now, death didn't claim David Livingstone that year. Henry Morton Stanley, commissioned by the *New York Herald* to find him, arrived at Ujiji on 23rd November.

David was startled as one of his men ran into his hut to tell him the news that a white man was coming into the village. Slowly he heaved himself to his feet, put on the only decent jacket and hat he still had and went out. A few moments later the historic meeting between Stanley and Livingstone took place.

It proved David's salvation, for under the care of the journalist—explorer he gradually regained his health.

Eventually they went their separate ways—as you can read in the chapter on Henry Morton Stanley—with Livingstone more interested than ever in solving the problem that intrigued him most, the riddle of the River Lualaba.

In mid-August—the middle of the rainy season, during which he had never started a journey—Livingstone set out southwards

This time he was not at prayer. The great explorer was dead.

to Lake Bengueolo. It seemed a march doomed from the beginning. Within a few weeks, the fever started to attack him again, sapping all the energy he had so laboriously regained.

Slowly, oh, so terribly slowly, he made progress, taking several months to reach the Bengueolo. Even then, he wanted to go farther, and, in fact, set out. But, within a few days, he held up his arm, calling a halt. Carried on a stretcher, as he now was, he knew it was folly to go on. He ordered his men to return to the nearest village.

Citambo it was called, and a more miserable little place they could not have reached that 1st May in 1873. But hastily his men prepared as comfortable a hut as possible for the old explorer.

Breathing painfully, his eyes half shut, he was helped on to a rough couch that his faithful servants Susi and Ciuma had prepared. As evening neared, he appeared a little better and asked his two servants to leave him alone for a while.

A strange, sad silence seemed to hang over the village and over the hut in which the dim light of a candle flickered. In the middle of the night, Susi, moving silently as a cat, entered the hut to see if there was anything his master needed.

David Livingstone was kneeling beside his couch, his face concealed in his hands in parayer—a last prayer—a prayer that had ended a little time earlier. David Livingstone was dead.

His men filed into the hut one by one to take a last look at their master, and then they embalmed his body, before carrying it towards the sea where they handed it over to other white men to take back to a last resting place in David Livingstone's homeland.

He lies today in Westminster Abbey—the last resting place of many of Britain's greatest men.

VASCO DA GAMA

Through the rolling, tossing seas ploughed the tiny Portuguese ships . . .
seeking the route to India that had eluded men for centuries

Backwards and forwards across the royal chambers paced King Manuel I of Portugal and his counsellors. Worry was etched on every face, for the future greatness of their country was at stake.

"These Arabian and Venetian merchants are a plague upon us," scowled the king. "All the spices and riches of India are theirs for the taking, and there is not a thing we can do about it. Is there no way we can capture this trade and bring to our country even greater magnificence than is hers already?"

As the 15th century neared its close, every nobleman and merchant in Portugal knew the answer to the king's question. What was needed was a trade route to the East by sea. When an ounce of pepper was worth almost its weight in gold, getting a hold on the spice trade was of the most vital importance.

What made the matter even more urgent was that Portugal's great traditional rival, Spain, had the same idea in mind. Both countries meant to be first to find that sea route to the East.

Both had conceded that neither could snatch away the existing monopoly already held upon the trade by the Arabs and Venetians, who had long since found routes to India of their own and guarded them jealously.

Costly and ruinous wars awaited Portugal and Spain if they attempted to further their trade by battle.

Despair gripped Portugal in 1492 when it was learned that Spain had sent three ships to find the elusive sea route. Commanded by Christopher Columbus, whose name was to be carved forever in the pages of history, the tiny caravels had ploughed their way out into the unknown seas—and both Spain and Portugal expected his triumphant return.

And certainly it was a triumphant homecoming. Not because he had achieved what he had set out to do, find a new route to India, but because he had discovered the new and unknown continent of America.

Admittedly he had not returned with immediate treasures for Spain's awaiting coffers, but he had gained for her a vast new overseas empire.

Already Spain had gained the promise of prestige and power from the discovery of her new lands abroad, and soon, no doubt, those lands would bring her gold, silver, spices and other precious goods that might increase her wealth.

All this only served to increase the helpless fury of Manuel of Portugal. Not only had his country's greatest and nearest rival achieved new glory, but she was still scanning the seas for the trade route to India.

What if Spain also found that first? How would Portugal ever hold high her head again? Come to that—in a sense— she might not even have a head to hold high much longer.

By 1497, Manuel and his ministers were desperate. Portugal had tried and tried, and still fortune had not smiled on her.

Portuguese ships had sailed down the coasts of West Africa seeking a passage between the Atlantic Ocean and Eastern waters. They had ventured boldly from cape to cape, touched upon and discovered new islands, spotted new rivers, identified and explored them. Whole new maps had been drawn by their ambitious and audacious seafarers.

Henry the Navigator, who lived from 1394 to 1460, had rightly earned his nickname for the way in which he had promoted Portuguese exploration and discovery. With the impetus and inspiration given to his country's seamen by Henry, the Portuguese reached the Madeira Islands, Cape Bojador, Cape Blanco, Cape Verde and the mouth of the Gambia.

Bartholomew Diaz had helped carry on Henry's fine traditions. In one of the most epic seagoing voyages of all time he had sailed down the entire west African coast and rounded its southern headland into the Indian Ocean without at first even realising it.

So storm-tossed and terrifying was that voyage in 1488 that he had named his last cape the 'Cape of Storms.' The name was changed by his king—then John II—on the return of Diaz. From then on it would be called the "Cape of Good Hope", said the monarch, for was there not now good hope that they might reach India?

But nine years had passed, and still that hope had not been realised. Small wonder that Manuel grew hot-tempered and clenched his fists in anger at the very mention of India.

"Now! Now or never!" he thundered at last. "We shall find this accursed route to India or my wrath shall be as boundless as the seas that keep us from it!"

He bent over every report and chart available, summoned one adviser after another, and then announced that an expedition must leave at the first available opportunity.

"And to whom will you entrust the leadership of this great enterprise?" inquired one of the king's ministers.

He needed to be a man of many parts—sailor, soldier and diplomat first. He needed to be young, for the voyage would be hard and long. He must be clever, and capable of using his own initiative; a fine leader of men; and a man who could command prestige in whatever part of the world.

And Portugal had such a man. His name was Vasco da Gama.

A knight of the royal house, he was passing the king's chambers when Manuel called out to him. At once he hastened towards his sovereign and stooped on bended knee.

"I would be very grateful if you could accept a service I am about to ask you," said Manuel, "It is one that will give you, I am certain, many worries and troubles in executing it".

"Whatever choice your Majesty has deigned to make rewards me deeply for my works and troubles," answered Vasco da Gama, kissing the hand of the king, and without

They had not seen land
for thirteen weeks—
a record in 1497—
but suddenly a shoreline
was seen on the horizon.

even asking the nature of his mission before accepting it.

Born in Sines, Estremadura in 1469, Vasco da Gama came from an ancient and noble family that already had given Portugal many warriors and navigators. Seafare and warfare were already in his blood.

Plans were discussed, and naturally Vasco consulted Bartholomew Diaz. Then the young adventurer was shown his fleet of four ships and 170 men, among whom were twelve under sentence of death, who might be used for particularly dangerous missions.

Vasco stared at the three caravels designed especially by Diaz – the *Gabriel* and the *Raphael*, 120 tons each, and the *Berrio*, almost a toy by comparison, of 50 tons. The fourth vessel was but a sea-going beast of burden, intended only to carry provisions before being sunk or abandoned.

Dawn was breaking on 8th July, 1497, when Vasco da Gama emerged from an abbey at Restello, near Lisbon, where he had spent the night with friends and monks. He marched proudly to his flagship, the *Gabriel*, and went aboard.

A short time later, the first orders were shouted through the still morning, anchors were weighed clanking aboard, timbers creaked, rigging flapped, and the four ships moved slowly down the last stretch of the river Tago towards the sea. Soon they were no more than specks on the shimmering horizon.

So intense was the jealousy among the sea-faring nations in the 15th century that records of expeditions were as closely guarded as state secrets. In fact, so skilfully do they appear to have been hidden that even today they have not turned up, so we cannot tell how Vasco sailed the early part of his voyage so successfully. But of one thing we are sure, Vasco had been briefed well, for of what we know about the early part of the voyage his navigation was almost faultless.

Avoiding the coast of Guinea and the west coast of Africa with their headwinds and contrary currents, he sailed far out across the Atlantic, next using the South-East trade winds to take him almost within sight of Brazil. Next the steered South by East until he picked up the Westerlies, which carried him to a bay he named St. Helena Bay, a mere hundred miles north of the Cape of Good Hope.

In that mammoth feat of seamanship, he was out of sight of land for 13 weeks—a record in 1497.

Few of the crews had cause to enjoy that first part of the voyage. As the ships headed south for the Equator, the men suffered from the heat and longed for fresh, cooling breezes. When they finally did encounter those, they found them more troublesome than the Equatorial heat.

The waters grew colder, massive patches of mist would descend like clammy sheets around the ships, which would lose sight of each other, often having to ring bells, sound trumpets or fire cannons to make their whereabouts known.

The rains became frequent and torrential, on occasions the weather bombarded the tiny fleet with hailstones, and often the men had to face freezing sleet driven at them from the Antarctic farther south.

Having replenished their supplies of water at St. Helena Bay, Vasco's ships nosed eastwards and only a few days later spotted the boundless black line of the African coast.

Perhaps it might do no harm to land and try to win the friendship of the natives, thought Vasco. Long afterwards, he must have pondered over the wisdom of that decision, for one encounter proved chilling.

As the first few sailors rowed to land, they were attacked by stones and spears and put to flight. Vasco da Gama himself was hit by one of the spears. The wound itself was no more than a scratch, but the crews had been warned by previous voyagers that Africans often poisoned the tips of their arrows and spears which caused agonising death within a few minutes.

Massive storms tossed the tiny ship as they rounded the Cape of Good Hope.

All eyes were on Vasco as he stared at the scratch. No expression on his face belied his emotions as he waited through what might be his last few minutes alive. A sigh of relief swept through the crews as eventually he shrugged, smiled and walked away. Fortune had favoured him.

Within sight soon was the tip of Africa—and the Cape of Good Hope about which they had been warned. Nor had the warnings been exaggerated. The ships were tossed like tiny corks as massive storms battered them through waves that looked like moving mountains and gales hurled the crews furiously against the timbers.

For three long weeks they were at the mercy of that maelstrom before thankfully they dropped anchor in Mossel Bay where the crews fell exhausted on the decks, many of them too weak to move another muscle.

By this time, though, it was not merely exhaustion from fighting the storms from which they were suffering. The seaman's curse of scurvy—that weakening, killing complaint caused by lack of fresh fruit and vegetables—had taken its toll.

Vasco knew that courage alone was not enough to keep his crews going. They needed a long rest and fresh food if they were to press on, and they remained at Mossel Bay until mid-December, regathering their strength and will, though only half-heartedly.

Christmas that year proved dismal and depressing. Gloom hung over the three caravels—by now the supply ship had been burned—and Vasco had grave decisions to make.

Did they stay where they were, try to return or carry on?

It was impossible to turn back now, he knew. And further rest would accomplish nothing. He had to force his way forward again, praying fervently for success.

The three ships sailed again into a New Year that seemed determined to mock their puniness with titanic storms and tempestuous winds. They could get no farther than the delta of the Zambesi.

By now the resentment of the men was growing serious. Mutiny seemed to stand waiting like an enormous powder keg, and needed only the tiniest spark to ignite it.

Vasco acted decisively. The more troublesome sailors were clapped in irons, and then dramatically he picked up compasses, instruments and charts, strode to the side of the ship and hurled everything overboard.

"From this point on," he declared, "God alone will lead our ships. Place your trust in his mercy."

The men murmured among themselves and started to disperse in groups to perform their duties. The immediate crisis was ended.

Vasco's dramatic act was not as foolhardy as it appeared. He had already memorised the course he meant to take. And—more than that—he had noticed among the natives that some wore turbans.

Obviously then these natives must have made contact with Arabs, whose head dress the turban was. Surely he was on the right course now. Surely he could not be far from those coasts along which Arab merchant ships plied.

In March, 1498, scattered groups of huts appeared along the coasts. And then they saw a town, a real port, bustling with activity, people scurrying about the quays, boats coming to and fro. Vasco's tiny Portuguese fleet had reached Mozambique.

If they expected a welcome, they were sadly mistaken. Ostensibly the merchants and leaders of the town greeted them with friendship, offered them supplies and agreed to provide a pilot who would guide the Portuguese to India. But somehow there was hostility in the air. Vasco da Gama had a sixth sense for danger and recognised simmering threats veiled behind smiling faces.

It was as well that he did, for the Arabs had been alarmed by

Now Vasco knew he was nearing his objective. Some of the natives he met wore turbans— sure sign that they had been in contact with Arabs.

35

the sudden appearance of the three caravels. Soon more ships would start to come, they realised, and Arab trade would be undermined. They wanted rid of these Christian intruders.

There was no question of blasting them from the sea. The three Portuguese ships were too powerful for that. And so a more devious plan was hatched.

Guided by native pilots, Vasco's ships were to be driven on to jagged rocks and sent to the bottom.

"Keep your eyes wide open," said the suspicious Vasco to his brother Paul, who commanded the *Raphael*, and to his old friend Nicolao Coelho, who captained the *Berrio*.

They had little trouble in thwarting the Arabs, and took no reprisals against the treacherous town, though as they sailed away from Mozambique, their cannons pointed menacingly at the port . . . warning for the future.

Though frustrated, the Arabs were already on their way to pass on warnings of their own. Fast dhows sped to Mombasa, the next port of call, and hasty consultations were held there to plan the downfall of the Portuguese.

This time the Arabs decided to attack. Their plan was to board the ships silently and massacre the crews.

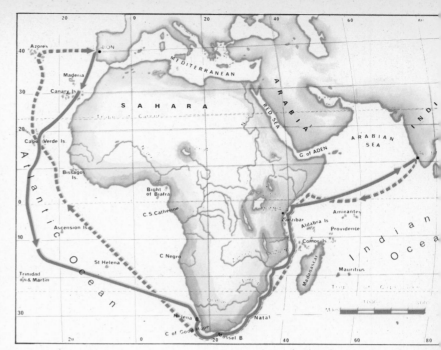

Although they knew the Portuguese ships were unassailable as far as open battle was concerned, their crews were sick, undernourished, utterly exhausted, dispirited by the deaths of companions, homesick and uncertain of their future. A sneak attack at night would be easy.

Vasco found the usual friendly welcome awaiting when his ships reached port. But, as before, he sensed hostility.

When a number of Arabs asked to come aboard his ships, he refused permission, except to a very few. When the Sheikh of Mombasa sent an envoy to invite the 'Christian admiral' to his palace, Vasco answered that he could not leave his ship. To his crews he passed his message: "Be careful of the night."

The watches were doubled; and suddenly in the flitting shadows the shapes of tiny craft were seen knifing silently towards the motionless caravels.

"Fire!" The command rasped out, and heavy cannons thundered in the night. Blazing boats were hurled from the water and within moments the Arabs were scuttling swiftly back to safety.

As dawn broke, Vasco headed out to sea. He would try elsewhere to find the hand of friendship.

Only a few miles up the coast he did find it. In the port of Malindi, on 14th April, he received a warm and genuine welcome from the sultan, a sworn enemy of the sheikhs of Mozambique and Mombasa. His hospitality was overwhelming, and soon Vasco's weary crews were well on their way to recovery.

But, most important of all, it was at Malindi that Vasco was introduced to Ahmed ibn Majid, the most famous Arab navigator of the time, who readily agreed to pilot the little Portuguese fleet across the great Indian ocean.

With the summer monsoon winds blowing steadily against their square sails, Vasco's ships ploughed steadily eastwards. And in less than a month they saw land.

It was India, the land of spices—their longed-for-goal. Vasco had achieved for Portugal what Columbus had failed to do for Spain. On 20th May, 1498, he dropped anchor in Calicut—a town on the west coast of India—and lowered himself to his knees in prayer.

It would have been a far happier ending to the story had their landing been splendid and popular—but instead the Portuguese received a rude shock.

Information they had received in Mombasa—which perhaps they should have known better than believe—had led them to assume Calicut would be peopled by no more than savages.

Instead they found a thriving port, well organised to cope with the spice trade from the East to Europe, ruled by an Indian rajah whose wealth defied description.

Vasco stared in dismay at the cheap trinkets he had brought as goodwill presents and realised with horror what a terrible mistake he had made.

The Portuguese were treated with contempt wherever they went, snubbed by the ruler and abused and stoned by the Arab merchants whose trade they had come to take away.

Rather hastily Vasco and his ships put out to sea again, only their big cannons keeping threatening Arab dhows at bay.

And what a nightmare voyage the return turned out to be. Ill-provisioned, the ships were ravaged again by scurvy. The crews faced starvation and death from thirst. On top of that, they knew they must face those roughest of rough seas again.

Battered beyond repair, the *Raphael* was abandoned and burned, while the remaining two ships limped back to Lisbon on a hope and a prayer, finally dropping anchor on 11th July, 1499.

Manuel was delighted. Portugal was joyous. Banners flew and trumpets blasted out the triumph of the magnificent Vasco da Gama.

The men who would make that same voyage to India in the future—Portugal knew—would somehow overcome the initial hostility and open up great trading posts that would enormously increase the spice trade between the two continents.

But most important was that they would be able to go at all. Vasco da Gama had seen to it that they could—his dedication to his king, and his courage in the face of terrible difficulties had ensured that those who followed him would be certain of reaching what before had been an unknown world.

**King Manuel was delighted.
Portugal was joyous.
Vasco da Gama had
returned with wonderful news.**

HENRY MORTON STANLEY

THE HARD-EYED NEWSPAPERMAN
WHO CONQUERED THE CONGO

I daresay you have heard of David Livingstone, haven't you?" asked James Bennett, the dynamic editorial director of the *New York Herald*, who was sitting in his Paris office.

"Of course," came the answer from the equally dynamic journalist, seated across the desk from him. "Who hasn't? Just about a legend in his own lifetime, isn't he?"

Henry Morton Stanley—a hard-eyed, no-nonsense, special newspaper correspondent—rhymed off a few facts about the great missionary and explorer who had spent most of his life in Central Africa. By now the grand old man was getting on in years, cut off from the world somewhere in the vast black continent.

For all anyone knew, Livingstone might no longer be alive. And whether or not he was still going strong was what Bennett wanted to know. With a good editor's nose for the unusual and unexpected story, James Bennett smelt a scoop somewhere. That was why he had sent for Stanley.

"Doctor Livingstone, I presume."
These were probably the best remembered
words in the history of exploration.

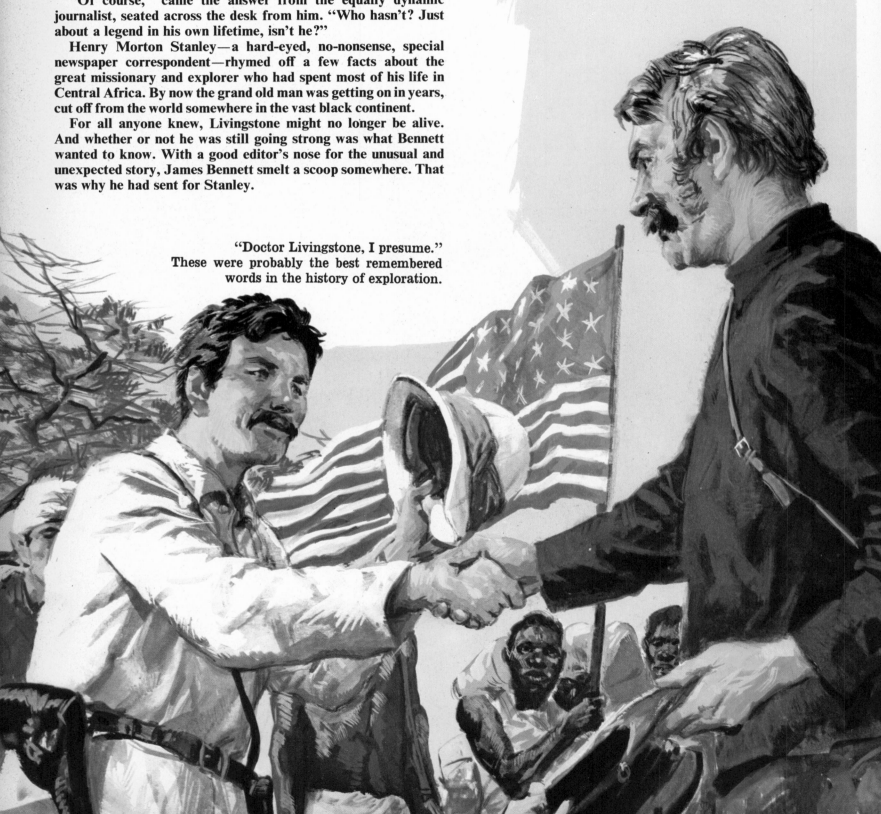

"Where do you think Livingstone is right now?" he asked, settling back in his chair, fixing piercing eyes on the 28 year old newspaperman.

Stanley thought for a moment, then shook his head slowly. "Honestly haven't an idea, sir."

"Do you think he's still alive?"

"Perhaps. Perhaps not. Who knows?" He shrugged.

"Well," said Bennett, now leaning forward, his eyes fixed on Stanley's face, "I know the very man who's going to find out. You are. I'm sending you to Africa, to track him down."

"Fine," replied Henry Morton Stanley in a calm voice that disguised his surprise at this latest assignment.

But that was all part of the character of the young journalist. He had come up through life the hard way, and it was not in his nature to show either fear or surprise, or any emotion in the face of a challenge.

If people can be said to serve an apprenticeship in life, Henry Morton Stanley had served one of the very hardest.

Born John Rowlands on 28th January, 1841, in Denbighshire, Wales, he lived through a childhood so drab and desperate that trying to forget it was about the only mercy it ever afforded him. Most of his boyhood was spent behind the forbidding walls of a heartless orphanage. Finally he could stand it no more and made his escape one dark night, determined to make his own way in the world.

He was ready to do anything to eke out an existence, and he went from one job to another to prove it. He travelled from town to town as a pedlar, risked his limbs as an acrobat in travelling circuses and sideshows, took one labouring job after another and served as a cabin-boy at sea.

Sailing the seven seas eventually took him to New Orleans in America, and even as he landed in that growing new continent, he was on his way to trouble. His arrival there was but a few years before the outbreak of the American Civil War, in which he was forced to fight for the Confederates, suffered grave wounds and was taken prisoner.

For anyone down on his luck, the aftermath of that terrible war was a very unpleasant time to be alive. And Stanley seemed fated to be down on his luck. He wandered aimlessly, rode the freight trains from place to place in search of any job that would earn him a few cents to quell the rumblings of his often starving stomach. Occasionally he went back to sea, working as the lowest deck hand, to stay alive.

All this and more he put up with, yet it did not entirely dampen his spirit. Somehow he kept alive a determination not to surrender to hopelessness, saying to himself time and again that one day his fortunes would change.

And one day they did. As he walked down the gangplank after one particularly dreary sea voyage he swore to himself that there and then he would make a final and definite break with the past.

First thing he did was change his name from John Rowlands to Henry Morton Stanley—the name of a man in New Orleans who had been the only person ever to show him any friendship—and then he vowed he would never take any back-breaking job again.

Of one thing he did feel certain—that he could write. And from then on he determined to make his living with the pen. Succeed he did, in the most spectacular fashion. Within a few years he had become one of the most popular special correspondents in the whole of the United States. That was why Bennett sent for him in his bid to find Livingstone.

Zanzibar was where most African travellers made for first. That was Stanley's starting point as well, and on 21st March, 1871, he set out at the head of a party of 192 men.

For over seven months they pushed their way forward through that friendless territory—hacking their way through matted jungle, pressing on across savannah burnt by the sun, or wading over plains flooded by the equatorial rains.

The hardened newspaperman proved a cruel pacemaker. Harsh with himself and severe with his men, he was rarely satisfied with the progress he made. But the one thing he never lacked in those lands so unfamiliar to him was courage.

Whatever the dangers of Africa—visible or invisible—Stanley took them in his stride. He fought off savage, attacking tribes of natives, scorned the wildest animals with contempt, brushed away disease-carrying insects with irritated flicks, refused to give into fever or worry about the fouled, polluted waters that often barred his way.

And all the time he kept asking anyone they met for news of the 'old white man'. More often than not, the answers he received were vague or contradictory.

Fatigue had drawn in his face, and there were slight signs of disheartenment in his manner on 10th November, when they reached Ujiji—a run-down old trading post on the shores of Lake Tanganyika. He strolled along the dirty, narrow, makeshift streets of the tiny village, ready to ask more questions of the natives, when his head jerked up at the sound of a cheery voice.

"Good morning, sir." That was all he heard. But he swung round, his face a portrait of astonishment.

Standing there, smiling broadly, was a black man, wearing the snowiest white shirt Stanley had seen in months. "Who are you?" he asked.

"My name is Susi, sir. I am the servant of Dr. Livingstone."

"What?" replied Stanley, his eyes widening, his mouth falling

More than once Stanley was engaged in fierce clashes with native tribes—
and later was criticised heavily for trail-blazing with the gun.

open in surprise. "You mean Dr. Livingstone is here?"

"Why, yes, sir."

Stanley didn't know whether to start jumping up and down in delight. But, hardened veteran of many emotional moments, he controlled himself, even appearing unmoved as his eyes glanced down the street and took in that next momentous sight.

Pale and tired-looking, an old man, surrounded by a small crowd of Arabs, was walking his way.

Stanley began to walk forward, too, his eyes fixed on the figure before him. At last they stood face to face, and Stanley took off his hat before speaking the words that are now immortal.

"Dr. Livingstone, I presume."

"Yes."

"I thank God for granting that I should see you," said Stanley, gripping the old man's hand warmly and shaking it.

"And I am happy to be here to receive you," chuckled Livingstone, his lined face breaking into a gentle, kindly smile.

The young newspaperman had reached his goal and achieved his finest moment. But then he looked at the famed explorer again. Sympathy flooded through him. The old man was sick and tired, and he was in great need of assistance. There and then

Stanley decided he would not leave until Livingstone was in sounder health. For four months, he stayed with him, gradually nursing the kind old doctor back to health.

During that time, the two men talked tirelessly, and Henry Morton Stanley was held fascinated by Livingstone's accounts and experiences of Africa.

He talked about his travels, told what he had found, expressed his doubts about some things and his hopes about others. Some questions he felt he had answered. Others he had not.

Now one question above all intrigued him. He wanted to know more about a great river the natives called Lualaba, a wide and winding waterway which seemed interminable in its majestic flow.

"But where does it flow?" asked Livingstone. "To the sea? And, if so, which sea? The Mediterranean? The Atlantic? Or is it perhaps part of the basin of the Congo or the Niger or the Nile? Might it not even be one of these three rivers?" he puzzled.

In the four months they stayed together, Stanley and Livingstone went out on a few minor treks of their own, paying particular attention to Lake Tanganyika, mapping and charting it.

But at last came the time for them to part. Livingstone wanted

"Lady Alice"

to plunge further into the dark interior of Africa, while Stanley felt it was about time that he made his way back to the coast to file his story for the world that Livingstone was alive and well.

On his return to civilisation, Stanley's reception turned out to be anything but rapturous. He was granted recognition and rewards for what he had achieved, certainly, but otherwise his taste of fame was sour indeed.

Many people openly abused him for revealing the results of Livingstone's explorations. They accused him of trying to steal the old man's glory. Others berated him for the way he had treated the natives in his party.

Stanley did not answer the criticisms. He seemed neither to care about them, nor to show the slightest further interest in Africa, apart from publishing his book *How I Found Livingstone* in 1872. He simply carried on with his job as a journalist.

But Africa had taken possession of his soul. Stanley wasn't saying so, but the Dark Continent was calling him back.

In 1873, he heard the news that Livingstone had died, and it was then that the newspaperman with the 'heart of iron' felt the call of Africa almost as strongly as some supernatural command.

"Suddenly," he wrote, "I felt inflamed with a decision to take up Livingstone's work; to be, if God wanted me to, another martyr of geographical science or, if I could be spared, to solve not only the problems of the Lualaba, but also those aspects still in doubt and incomplete in the discoveries of Burton, Speke, Grant . . ."

Sponsored by both the *Daily Telegraph* and the *New York Herald*, he then selected three trustworthy companions—brothers Frank and Edward Pocock, and a geologist named Frederick Barker—and set sail for Zanzibar, which they reached in the autumn of 1874.

With them they took the *Lady Alice*, which was to prove an admirable and indispensable aid in their adventures. Made of cedarwood, this was a boat, almost forty feet long, which could be dismantled into five sections and carried easily on the shoulders.

Despite those earlier criticisms of severity and cruelty, many of the men who had accompanied Stanley on his famous trip to find Livingstone were eager to offer their services for this latest expedition. But even they, familiar with the drive and relentless pace that this man could set, were taken aback when they heard what he intended to do and how much ground he intended to cover.

"Master," they cried, this long journey will take years—six, nine, ten years."

"Rubbish!" exploded Stanley. The Arabs take two years to reach Ujiji. I took—going and coming back—only eighteen months. Remember?"

Stanley met Tippu Tib, a strange Arab adventurer who traded in ivory and slaves.

"Yes, yes."

"Very well then. I assure you I have not come to Africa to stay."

On 17th November, the expedition left Bagamoyo; 356 people started that march, and 173 of them were not to come back.

Among the first to die was Edward Pocock, who fell victim to typhus. Stanley kept his grief to himself and insisted that the expedition press on.

On 27th February, 1875, he reached Lake Victoria, around which he immediately started to sail aboard the *Lady Alice*. Hazardous and alarming that undertaking turned out to be, made all the more dramatic by frequent confrontations with hostile tribes on the banks. But, at the end, it was clear that only one river, the Kagera, entered the lake, and only one river, the Nile, came out of it.

After 56 days, Stanley returned to his base camp and found his men waiting for him in small groups on the shore. Among them stood Frank Pocock, but there was a sad, strained look on his face. Stanley knew something was wrong, and he thought he knew what.

"Where is Barker?" he asked quietly. "Why isn't he here?"

The answer he half expected came. "He died twelve days ago." Once more a pall of gloom fell over the expedition.

Nevertheless, Stanley meant to press on—this time towards Uganda. And there he met King Mtesa who, now converted to the Moslem religion, was no longer the bloody tyrant described by John Hanning Speke.

The intrepid newspaperman hacked onwards through the most difficult territory.

that the journey was far too dangerous. There were crocodiles, waterfalls, rapids, and tribes of cannibals.

However, lured by the promise of 5,000 dollars reward, he and his band finally agreed to join the expedition, which set out again on 5th November, 1876.

For more than a month they made their way down the Lualaba, passing through thick forests, touching lost villages, often opening up a way with guns among especially savage tribes.

But on 12th December, Tippu Tib, tired of walking sailing and fighting, asked Stanley for his leave and his 5,000 dollars. The explorer had no choice but to pay him and let him go.

Suddenly he was all alone with just his own men, facing the obscure enigma of the great river. Nevertheless, Stanley and his surviving companion, Frank Pocock, hardened their determination to push on to the end, whatever the risks.

Their survey of the Lualaba lasted from 26th December 1876 to 12th August, 1877 and was one of the most fascinating, dangerous and glorious adventures in the history of exploration.

The farther Stanley proceeded and the more he took bearings, the more he became convinced that the Lualaba was neither the Nile nor the Niger.

Was it the Congo then? He felt almost certain. And his certainty was confirmed by the words of an old leader from the village of Rubunga.

"I asked him", wrote Stanley, "in a mixture of languages, the name of the river. After a few moments he answered, "Ibari". But once he understood the real sense of the question, he exclaimed, "Ikutu ya Kongo."

The final great mystery of Africa was a mystery no longer. It was another glorious moment in the history of exploration.

But with the triumph came tragedy.

Hardly able to walk, because of a bad infection in his feet, Frank Pocock attempted to cross a river upstream near its shallows. Sadly there was a whirlpool nearby, and Pocock lost his footing and his life as he vanished forever beneath the churning waters.

About a month later, Stanley reached the Atlantic Ocean and gained legendary fame.

His magnificent journey—described by him in his famous book *Through The Dark Continent*—earned for him the highest acclaim and the greatest praise.

But, as had been the case after his expedition to find Livingstone, he was pelted again by the brickbats of public opinion. A few years later he was back in Africa.

Commissioned in 1879 by King Leopold of Belgium to further exploration and build roads and river stations in the Congo, he worked hard there for almost five years, helping to lay the foundations of the Free State of the Congo, later to be called the Belgian Congo.

He visited Africa yet again in 1887, on a mission similar to that which had first taken him to the great continent—to find a man who had vanished there: a German ambassador, Dr. Schnitzer, also known as Emin Pasha, who had been cut off from the world during a rebellion.

On an expedition even more dangerous and drastic than those before, Stanley finally found his man and persuaded him, though with some difficulty, to leave the by then troubled land.

Finally the journalist-turned-explorer ended his wanderings, settling down at his homes in London and Surrey.

Later he became a member of Parliament from 1895 to 1900.

By the time of his death on 10th May, 1904 he had added another word to the name he had adopted in New Orleans. Granted a knighthood, he had become Sir Henry Morton Stanley.

Thanks to his help, Stanley was able to sail right round Lake Tanganyika and study its every detail. It was soon made clear in his mind that the lake was no part of the Nile Basin. He had now established beyond all doubt that Burton was wrong and Speke right.

By the end of 1876—after two years hard and exhausting journeying—Stanley faced the final problem. This was the one that tugged at his curiosity most, the mystery that had so pre-occupied David Livingstone—that of the River Lualaba.

If he could solve this mystery, Stanley felt that he would have completed the work of Livingstone and laid bare forever the last great secret of Central Africa.

And so started yet another long trek, which finally brought them to Nyangwe, the most northerly point ever reached by Livingstone on the Lualaba.

Here it was that Stanley met the band of Hamed bin Mhamed —called Tippu Tib—a strange Arab adventurer, an ivory and slave merchant. Tippu Tib, "tall, with a black beard, stiff and quick in his movements, nervously moving eyes, very white teeth", listened to Stanley's questions about the Lualaba only to answer that he had no idea where the river led.

"But in which direction does it flow?" pleaded Stanley. "Does it continue north?"

"It continues north."

"And the sea? Is that to the north too?"

"Only God knows," came the reply.

Stanley asked Tippu Tib if he would accompany him along the Lualaba for sixty days, at which the adventurer answered

ERIC THE RED

Because of a fierce and fiery temper, the young Viking was banished from his own shores . . . but sailed unafraid through the stormiest seas to discover new and unknown lands.

Young Viking boys didn't cry. Sons of ferocious, war-faring fathers, they were brought up to be brave. But possibly ten-year-old Eric struggled to fight back a tear or two as he strode alongside his father to the rough shore and sturdy boat moored there.

Never again was he to see his home, he knew that. Banished forever from the land of his birth, he was about to embark on a voyage into the unknown—condemned to plough through the cold, grey waters of the North Sea until he and his family found somewhere to settle, or those turbulent waters sucked them down into their gloomy depths.

Slowly the *knorr*—as Viking boats were called—nosed away from the Norwegian shores, its striped sail flapping at the wind.

On and on it sailed—the few men, women and children aboard often silently lost in thought—until as far as the eye could see there was nothing but the waves of the rolling sea capped with spattering crests of foam.

Young Eric stood at the stern. Every few moments he would brush away long locks of ginger hair, as the winds tossed his unkempt mop across his face. But he looked a fine little figure.

Now and again he glanced upwards at the tall, bearded man beside him, whose hand gripped the helm firmly, keeping the ship on a steady course.

Suddenly noticing the boy's glance, the father looked down with a quizzical smile.

"Well, Eric?" he asked in his growling voice. "You have realised where we are bound?"

"Yes, father. To the West. To Iceland."

"Are you afraid, my boy?"

"No, father," replied Eric, setting his shoulders more squarely. "I am my father's son. The blood of Vikings runs through my veins. I shall fear nothing."

Thorvald's weathered face broke into a smile. He nudged his ten-year-old son proudly, then returned his eyes once more to the horizon.

If Thorvald had any regrets about his banishment, he probably tried not to show them. But lingering in the back of his mind may have been many a longing for the land he had now left behind.

The year was about 960, and Thorvald had been a man of some property. Near the village of Jaederen—not far from Stavanger in modern Norway—he had owned a large farm, inherited from his father, Asvald.

He had worked hard on his lands, building the farm even bigger, filling his fields with more and more cattle and growing wealthy enough to employ a household of servants to do his every bidding.

But Thorvald had one great flaw in his character. He had a terrible temper. In an age when men were by nature hard, he was harder and more quarrelsome than most. At the slightest provocation, his hand would reach for his sword or mighty axe, and his wrath would erupt.

We cannot be certain whom he killed in a heated brawl. There is even the suggestion that he had slaughtered several men in a number of fights. But, in the opinion of the Viking elders, he had committed one murder too many and he had to be punished.

Exile for life was the sentence—and, in those troubled times, that was a punishment only a little less harsh than death itself. The banished had their homes and all their lands confiscated, were allowed to take away with them only what one sailing craft could carry, and then they were set loose in a world where the mere sight of a Viking invited suspicion and hostility.

For most banished men, there was only one way of life left. They became robbers, pirates and plunderers, scavenging what they could, living like hunted animals until either they were hacked down in a skirmish or died unwanted in some lonely, desolate spot.

Thorvald knew that he, too, might have to fight hard to survive, but to his credit, he was determined not to abandon his family as others before him had done. Somehow he meant to start again, build up a new life for himself and his family. He meant to settle in Iceland, discovered and colonised by his forefathers about eighty years previously.

His sturdy little *knorr* made its journey safely. One day Thorvald and young Eric looked westwards for the last time on that voyage and saw land ahead. They had reached their destination. But what lay in store for them now?

The only fertile lands lay along the coast. Behind loomed stark, forbidding mountains where it was certainly impossible to grow or rear cattle.

Not surprisingly, by the time Thorvald and his family arrived, the choicest lands had all been taken. As the banished travellers cruised along the coastline, they saw everywhere farms and fenced fields with herds of cattle grazing in the meadows. Spirals of smoke, curling lazily upwards from each home, revealed the presence of men.

Thorvald was forced to sail farther north towards chillier and less cheerful lands, but finally, at a place called Drangar, he found an unclaimed spot where his family could settle. The very day they landed, they began to build themselves a house and scour the countryside for some way of making a living.

Exactly how they fended for themselves from the start we do not know, but gradually as the years passed they made a living. They built a tiny farm, tilled a few crops and tended a small herd of cattle. Everyone was reasonably happy.

Well, no, not quite everyone. Eric, now growing into manhood, felt strong, and strange urges of restlessness stirred within him.

Under the guidance of his father, he had learned how to live off the land, and quite often they had gone out to sea together, which had made a fine sailor of Eric.

There were also other things he had learned from Thorvald. The red-haired young Viking could now wield a sword and axe with the best of men, and he had inherited his father's inclination to settle any quarrel with a strong arm.

As he continued to live in Drangar, however, he was seen often with a deep, brooding look in his eyes. For long periods he

Strong and brave, Eric the Red was admired by his Viking followers for his courage.

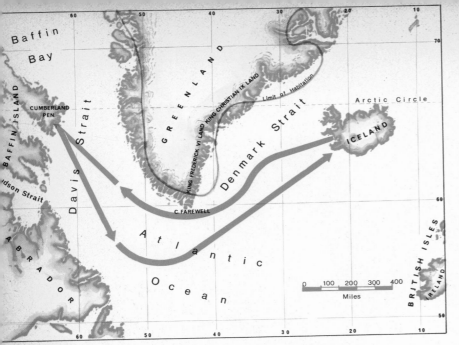

Eric's sword flashed, and men died under his sweeping blade.

would stare out to sea, while childhood memories came flooding back.

He recalled the tales of those hardy Vikings who had lived only for the sea. From Norway and from Iceland itself, many had set course east, south and west on exciting voyages of adventure. Many had never returned, he knew, but others had, often after long years away, and with them they had brought back stories that had held the young Eric spellbound.

A glorious, magnificent sight sprawled around him and his men. From one side, the boundless frozen wastes of Greenland stretched out like a carpet for as far as the eye could see. From the other, the blue, breathtaking waters of the sea rolled away into the distance.

But what did Eric care about beauty that day? He wanted plunder, and there was no sign of life anywhere. The land was miserable, desolate, hostile.

Suddenly one of his men cried out: "Land! I can see land westwards!"

Everyone gazed in the direction of his pointing arm, and, sure enough, on the very farthest horizon was the dark outline of another shore.

"To the boat!" shouted Eric. "The Westmen may be over there!" And before long, the Vikings were churning through the waters, their keen eyes peering ahead, waiting for that coastal outline to grow bigger, hoping the quest for their prey would be ended when they bounded down on to these other shores.

Another epic voyage was made, and, in 982, Eric the Red steered his *knorr* into yet another bay. Once more his hot temper boiled over, for again there was no sign of life.

What he failed to realise was that he had made yet another mark on history. He had set foot on a place we today call Baffin Island, part of a new continent that would not receive its present name until nearly five hundred years later.

Eric the Red had reached America.

But again the country was bleak and uncharitable. Near what is today's Cumberland Sound, he found nothing but frozen land, stark, craggy mountains and icy waters.

There was some compensation, however. The land was rich in Arctic wildlife, and they spent the summer hunting seals and walruses, foxes and bears. By autumn, burdened with valuable furs and tusks, they were ready to leave and sailed back to Greenland to spend the winter there.

As the spring of 984 budded into life, Eric's rugged *knorr* set out to sea yet again. This time he was bound eastwards. Back to Iceland. Back home. His punishment was over.

"Home? Was it really a home?" he thought, as he stood at the helm, watching the prow dip and rise in the spraying waters. Inside him was bubbling a strange brew of bitterness, pride and ambition.

"What kind of a home is Iceland?" he kept asking himself. "A wretched little land, too small for ambitious men," he answered. And had it not even banished him from its miserable shores? "Well, now I shall renounce Iceland," he vowed. "I shall build a new homeland in that country we have reached."

Eric had travelled far enough along those spartan coasts, but he had found that the interior of many fjords, protected from the north winds, supported green lands, fine pasturelands, ideal for growing cereals. The winters were long and hard, certainly, but so they were in Iceland.

He began to discuss his project with his companions, and they tried to think of a name for this new country.

"Call it Ericland," someone proposed. Eric shock his head.

"No," he said, "I will call it Green Land."

Everyone looked at each other in surprise. Green? Those

Banished from Iceland, Eric set sail for an unknown land said to exist in the West.

haggard mountains? Those grey cliffs?

Eric smiled, stroking his thick beard. "Yes, Green Land. Then, when they hear that name, men will come more willingly."

A cunning piece of guile on the part of Eric the Red, a sly trick perhaps to further the project in which he now believed so passionately—but that was how Greenland got the name it bears today, baptised so by a fearless, seafaring Viking.

On their return to Iceland, Eric and his companions planted the seeds of enthusiasm well. At once the red-haired Viking announced that he was taking his family, his cattle, his every-thing to this wonderful new land of plenty. His fellow sailors spoke just as passionately and began packing to leave.

Great waves of eagerness swept across Iceland's farms—and before long others were selling their lands and property to make the voyage to Greenland.

Eric settled at a place called Breidafjord, building there a fine farm with stables that could accommodate over fifty oxen. Gradually other colonists arrived at the virgin land—not without difficulty, it must be added, for the voyage was arduous, and many never reached Greenland at all.

Very few of them were angry that the land was not as green and fertile as Eric had said. Having arrived, no one wanted to go back, and they set to work with the will and determination that their forefathers had bred into them.

Windmills were put up, the first roads were built, and slowly but surely the colony began to thrive—not on a grand scale admittedly, but happily. By 1002, the Vikings in Greenland were said to number about a thousand.

And among them no one was held in higher esteem than Eric. "He enjoyed the greatest prestige," old chronicles tell us, "and whenever he passed, everyone used to bow before him . . . for at that time the men of Greenland were still pagans."

Exactly when he died is not known—some say he was among the victims of an epidemic that struck the colony—but Eric the Red passed into legend.

He also became a figure of controversy, and still is. Not everyone believes that the fiery-tempered, red-haired adventurer was the first man from the Old World to set foot on America. Whether Eric did or did not, however, few people now doubt that his son did.

"I saw a land, a green land edged with rocks. Beyond the rocks were woods and I saw game in them. But the storm forced me to turn from that shore and return to you."

A Council of elders listened in mounting excitement to the words of a young Viking named Bjarni who had unwittingly sailed near the coast of Newfoundland, and now they decided to send men in search of that land, because they needed wood in great quantities.

Chosen to lead that expedition was Leif, the son of Eric the Red, who, as we now know, reached his promised land, which he named Vinland because of the wild vines that grew there plentifully.

Almost 500 years later, Christopher Columbus was to be granted the lasting credit and acclaim for the discovery of America. But it seems as well that Eric the Red was not around by that time to dispute the claim. That burning fire within the hot-tempered Viking might have raged once more, and poor Christopher might have lost his head to the swing of an axe.

Some said they had found warm and fertile lands with prosperous settlements that they could pillage. Others talked of foggy islands, surrounded by seas rich with fish. Eric listened in fascination. But more gripping by far than any story he heard was that of the journey of Gunnbjörn, the young son of Ulf.

Gunnbjörn had voyaged westwards . . . westwards, where, as everyone knew, there was nothing but the open sea, until finally the edge of the world was reached.

Yet Gunnbjörn had sworn that was nonsense. He claimed that he had actually seen with his own eyes, among banks of fog that had suddenly opened, the profile of a rocky land.

That was long, long ago, and the elders had smiled with disbelief at Gunnbjörn's words. But not Eric, he hadn't mocked. Could there really be a new land somewhere out there? Might he one day seize his chance to set out in search of it?

For the time, it seemed not. Eric's life appeared inextricably bound to the land on which he lived and worked—moreso when his father Thorvald died, leaving him the farm.

Now strong and handsome, and a property owner at that, Eric the Red—as everyone called him because of his ginger mane of hair and bristling beard—was regarded as an eminently suitable husband for many a fine girl.

One in particular appealed to him—the beautiful daughter of a rich and respected family—and, after his marriage to her, Eric was able to leave Drangar and move southwards where he bought a larger and more prosperous farm.

But there is a well-known saying—like father, like son—and, in one respect, that could not have been truer of Thorvald and Eric.

The same fierce warlike blood of his father flowed through Eric's veins, and he had inherited the same blazing temper that tugged a sword from its scabbard within seconds.

Before he was twenty, he had killed a couple of men in a quarrel and been sentenced to a short exile. Ten years later, in one of those vendettas that frequently stained the North with blood, Eric flew into a terrible rage and wielded his axe with the fury of a whirlwind.

Exactly how many men he killed in that brawl is not recorded, but there were enough corpses strewn around to bring down the wrath of Viking justice on his head, and severe punishment.

Eric was sentenced to exile for three years. And it was one of the harshest kinds of exile of all. He was not allowed to take his family with him.

The dilemma pricked his mind like a thorn. What was he to do? Where was he to go?

Three years was not really long enough to think of building a new farm or anything. He could not spend the time in Norway, for he was the son of the banished Thorvald. There appeared to be only one option—to join up with one of the bands of other banished Vikings who plundered and pillaged savagely along the coasts.

Yet no sooner had he decided to become one of these marauding pirates than he dismissed the idea. Hadn't he once had a dream and ambition—to go in search of that mysterious land westwards?

The die was cast. He meant to sail in the long-ago wake of Gunnbjörn and set foot on that other country.

"Will twenty or more of you dare to come with me?" he shouted to all those younger Vikings in whose eyes burned the flame of adventure. "Will you brave these open seas and sail westwards to the great unknown?"

"Aye!" they clamoured. "Aye, we will voyage with you to the end of earth!" was their answer, for Eric the Red was well-liked and admired by many just for that fiery temperament that had put him in his present predicament.

On a spring morning in 981, their big-bellied *knorr*—made to withstand the angriest waves—glided from the safe haven of a bay in Iceland on its hazardous venture. Every man aboard knew he might never see his homeland again.

Navigation in those dark days was no easy task. Vikings did not have compasses, as we know them, though they could 'read' the skies, able on a clear day to determine more or less where they were by the height of the sun in the sky. If the day was cloudy, or cliffs of fog hung over the sea, they apparently used the "stone of sail"—a magnetic splinter which floated in a container of water and indicated points north and south.

We know nothing of the course Eric the Red and his companions took, but it would seem they were caught in the flow of the Gulf Stream which started to push the Viking *knorr* towards Greenland.

And there the land was one day—exactly as Gunnbjörn had said—its enormous cliffs overhanging the sea. Both excitement and awe welled up among the hardy adventurers.

Gunnbjörn had said other things about his early voyage. He had talked about smoke he had seen, smoke that came perhaps from the settlements of people the Vikings called the 'Westmen'.

No, it was not a land where a man could make a home, but the Vikings found plenty to hunt.

The spreading legends had said that these were explorers and adventurers from the distant isle of Ireland, who had emigrated years before to a remote western land where they had settled and changed their names to the Westmen.

Now before the eyes of Eric and his Viking companions stood villages built from stones and mud. Eagerly they swept towards the shore, but even before the hull scraped the bottom, exultation dissolved into disappointment. Not even the thinnest spiral of smoke suggested there was anything to pillage. The place had been abandoned long since.

It wasn't difficult to realise why after Eric and his men had decided to winter in this new land. The weather and winds were wild and bone-chilling, the land bleak and inhospitable. As soon as their *knorr* could take to sea again, they were only too glad to get away. Down and round the far-stretching coast they sailed, searching constantly for settlements they could pillage.

Not a single one did they spy, and their frustration mounted.

What they did not realise, however, was that they had made a mark on history. They became the first men to circumnavigate southern Greenland, doubling round what today is called Cape Farvel and heading north through the waters of the Davis Strait.

Somewhere along there Eric spotted a mountain, standing tall like a majestic sentinel at the edge of the land. At once, he made up his mind to climb it to see if he could spot any trace of the elusive Westmen from its peak.

JAMES COOK

THE DISCOVERER DISCOVERED BY
AN ECLIPSE OF THE SUN

Coal by the ton was being loaded aboard a ship moored at the dirty, bustling dockside of Whitby. But, for once, Mr. John Walker, prosperous merchant who owned several coal ships that plied between England and the Baltic, had his eyes fixed not on the work but on the young seaman who paced the deck thoughtfully.

"Fine boy," he thought. "Not very old, I know, but I'd say without doubt he's the finest sailor I've ever seen on any of my ships. Yes, youth or no youth, he deserves the opportunity."

He clapped his arm round the young man's shoulders and a broad smile spread over his face. "I imagine this will come as a big surprise to you, James, my boy. I know it's not two years since you joined me as a cabin-boy, but you've come a long way since then. Such a long way that I'm offering you command of one of my ships."

"That's extremely kind of you, sir," replied James Cook. And next moment the merchant's face fell. "Thank you very much. But I shall have to decline your offer." Walker gasped in disbelief.

"I'm sorry, sir. But today I enrolled in His Majesty's Navy."

The two shook hands, and 27 years old James Cook walked down the gangplank, ready to face whatever this fresh start life had in store for him.

"Strange," whispered Mr. Walker to himself, watching the slim, serious-faced figure vanish among the bustle of the quays. "Very strange."

He wasn't the first man to have said that about young James Cook, who was born on 27th October, 1728, in the village of Marton, near Cleveland, Yorkshire, because James Cook was not of a seafaring family. Son of a farm labourer, taught to read and write by his father's employer, James had become a clerk and book-keeper; and at the age of seventeen was to be found behind the desk of a large store in the small town of Staithes, keeping a close eye on the accounts.

But, whenever he had a few days off, it was to the sea he headed. Finally one day, his mind was made up. He went to Whitby in search of the first ship that would take him on.

That was when he made the acquaintance of Mr. John Walker, whom James was to impress so much within the next two years. It wasn't an easy life on the grimy boats. Nevertheless, James Cook knew he had found his true vocation. The sight of a port or a shoreline filled him with strange emotion. Life at sea also awakened greater ambitions in him.

He knew that if he were ever really to sail—sail, that is, to the Earth's most far-flung corners—it was not merely enough to love the sea, or gradually work his way up through the ratings until he acquired a little more responsibility.

If he were ever to command a worthwhile ship of his own, he needed to understand all the nautical skills, astronomy, mathematics and everything else that made a great seaman. So, in the winter months, he would be found engrossed in books and maps, taking off time to study how to make calculations, draw and to fix routes and points.

All this diligence had not gone unnoticed by Mr. Walker—who was to remain a friend for life—and it was why he had offered one of his ships to young Cook. But too late. Far too late. The young seaman's sights now were steadily fixed elsewhere.

On 17th June, 1755, he sailed aboard the *Eagle*, a sixty-gun warship, bound on a tour of duty, guarding His Majesty's seas. Within two years he was deck master of the sixty-four gun *Pembroke*, aboard which he took part in the naval campaign against the French along the St. Lawrence River and North American coasts.

His personal bravery was outstanding. Under the heaviest enemy fire, he strolled the decks calmly, issuing commands in an easy, relaxed voice, hardly giving a glance at the heavy fire to which they often were exposed.

And, war or no war, he continued with his great passion of studying the coasts they neared. More than once during naval battles, he was seen making reliefs, sketching out maps and testing the depths of the St. Lawrence, rendering invaluable service to his country's fleets.

At the end of the war, Cook joined the *Northumberland*, and later took part in the exploration of the coasts of Labrador, Nova Scotia and Newfoundland, making extraordinarily accurate maps and reliefs of those territories.

Nor did he confine himself solely to those tasks. He also made studies of the stars, astronomic observations so clear and accurate that they were brought to the attention of the Admiralty and scientific bodies who were impressed immensely.

It would not be frivolous to say that the stars and planets plotted the destiny of James Cook—for calculations at the time revealed that the planet Venus was to pass across the face of the Sun on 3rd June, 1769, an astronomical event that would not take place again for over a century.

The best vantage point for the eclipse was Tahiti, and the Royal Society asked the government to send an expedition there to study the phenomenon. They agreed readily and the mission was entrusted to the Royal Navy, who held long discussions about the ships and men they ought to send.

There was soon little doubt in anyone's mind about whom they should send—"that brilliant fellow Cook." Promoted to lieutenant in 1768, he was invited to select whatever ship he wanted and prepare everything for the voyage.

As it was to be a mission of peace and science, he considered it futile to use an expensive warship, so it was back to Whitby he went, to visit his old friend John Walker, from whom he bought a large three-masted coal ship, cleaned it up and christened it the *Endeavour*.

Promoted to lieutenant in 1768, James Cook made ready for his first great voyage of discovery.

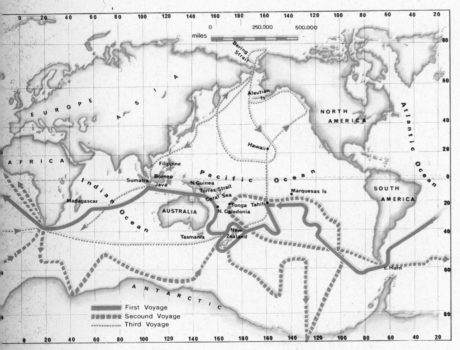

First Voyage
Secound Voyage
Third Voyage

On 25th August, 1768, she sailed from Plymouth with a crew of eighty men and a number of scientists. And low in the water the ship sailed, for her holds were well-stocked with vegetables and citrus fruits.

In those days, when scurvy ravaged the crews of most sea-going vessels, Cook, ahead of his time, felt convinced that the dread disease was caused by lack of fresh food.

The *Endeavour* reached Tahiti on 13th April, 1769, well in time to see the transit of Venus across the sun at 9.25 a.m. on 3rd June. As it was, the observations were unfortunately fouled by minor faults in the instruments and the scientists aboard were unable to achieve their main objective: that of calculating the distance of the Earth from the Sun.

"Having accomplished the envisaged observations," Admiralty orders said, "Sir, you will continue to 40° South to ascertain if at that latitude there is a continental land. If you do not find any land between 40° and 35°, go back West until you reach New Zealand. You will explore this land and return to England, following the route you will think more convenient."

"In the event you find a continent you will, with the greatest care and as extensively as possible, explore the coasts, drawing up maps of ports, bays and important routes for navigation. Furthermore, you will observe birds, fish, animals and the land. If there are mines or deposit of ores, you will take care to bring samples home, you will study with the greatest care the predisposition of the natives, if you find any, assessing their number, and trying to form a friendship with them."

And then the orders concluded, "Sir, with the agreement of the natives and in the name of the king, you will take possession of the most favourable territories."

Britain was still building her Empire at the time, and the Pacific Ocean promised rich pickings, for it was still largely unexplored.

Leaving Tahiti, where he had established good relations with the natives, Cook touched on the archipelago of the Society Islands, of which he took possession, and then caught sight of New Zealand in the early days of October.

By now the skies were grey and cloudy, holding the threat of hard autumn storms, but in the following six months, Cook took the *Endeavour* on a long cruise among the great islands, making exact drawings and confirming beyond all doubt that they were part of no continent nor—as someone had thought—a land attached to New Guinea.

Soon afterwards, Cook made one of the greatest discoveries in the building of Britain's empire—though the odd thing at the time was that he failed to realise it.

On 18th April, 1770, bound for Britain, the *Endeavour* reached the unknown shores of Australia's eastern coast and began to explore them.

It was probably one of the most hazardous pieces of navigation ever undertaken at the time—for that matter, at any time—for the presence of Australia's jagged, knife-pointed coral reefs made the progress of wooden-keeled boats not only dangerous but near suicidal.

On 10th June, 1770, Cook's log painted a vivid picture of the fate that might be awaiting them all.

"Night came," he wrote, "and the officers went to sleep. We were navigating with 17.21 fathoms under the keel, but towards eleven the depth reduced suddenly and before we could even measure the depth the ship ran aground with a terrible shudder."

Panic swept the *Endeavour*. What if she could not get out to sea again? Feverish, desperate work started which lasted for 24 hours.

"The ship was taking in water," reported the deck master, "and we immediately started to work with pumps while every heavy object was being thrown overboard: cannons, ballast and so on. The *Endeavour* was 50 tons lighter, but did not succeed in moving from the reef. And water was entering from the leak in such a way that I thought that if we did refloat, we would sink.

"The boats could not take all of us to the shore, and I was repeating to myself that during the shipwreck nobody would obey me and everybody would throw himself into the boats in a wild fight for life . . . the survivors would end up dying of thirst or in the pains of madness."

But luck was on the side of the *Endeavour*, which succeeded in refloating, while a piece of rock, partially shutting the leak, prevented the water invading the hold completely.

Through the Torres Strait, Cook managed to reach Java, where many of the men fell victims to malaria and dysentry, and it was a seriously decimated crew that finally brought back the *Endeavour* to Britain on 12th July, 1771.

The Admiralty was delighted with his voyage and findings, and rewarded him with the rank of commander. Possibly the only pity about that expedition was Cook's personal conviction that Australia was not a continent. It would have been a source of tremendous satisfaction to the intrepid adventurer to have realised in his own lifetime that he was the official discoverer of such a giant new land, having sailed into the bay where Sydney stands today.

His mind was already on a further voyage of exploration, which he proposed to the Admiralty. This time he wanted to go even farther south towards seas where the winds roared eternally like angry demons, and storms tossed ships like bottle-corks on mountainous waves engulfed in thick fogs.

Britain could not resist his tempting offer, for she was eager to know if there really existed that 'Southern Land' about which early explorers had brought back jumbled tales. Given two ships, the 462 tons *Resolution* and the 336 tons *Adventure*, Cook left Britain on 13th July, 1772.

Cook meant to make three great voyages this time. He intended to unravel the secrets of the Atlantic, thoroughly navigate the Indian Ocean and then make further examinations of the Pacific.

From the Cape of Good Hope, the southernmost tip of Africa, the ships were on their own, heading into the great unknown. Within weeks they were being buffeted by icy seas and storms far more angry than they had anticipated.

"At first I remained enchanted," wrote Cook, "in front of the sight of those floating blocks of ice, but then we were frightened because if waves threw us against those ice floes, the ships would break in hundreds of pieces."

Even so, Cook kept going. The polar circle was passed, the ships eventually arriving at 67° South. But here it became impossible to continue. Before the navigators stretched a boundless, grey barrier of ice. To make things worse, the two ships lost sight of each other. Anxious and alarmed, Cook ordered the helmsman to turn back towards New Zealand.

To his relief, Cook was re-united with the *Adventure* there,

Above all, Cook believed in establishing friendly relations with natives of the lands he discovered.

and for a while he granted himself and his men some rest. But by November, 1773, they were on their way again—sailing south once more.

Yet again the ships lost sight of each other in the blanketing fog, but bravely Cook nosed the *Resolution* onwards through erratic seas and their threatening icebergs, reaching 71° 10′ South on 30th January, 1774.

What appeared on the horizon were "clouds which had a strange brightness," caused by the reflection of the vast expanses of ice, Cook believed. At once he gave the orders to change course.

"I think that south, beyond the barrier of ice, there is a land. But, if there is, it cannot offer any more hospitality than the ice which undoubtedly covers it," he wrote. "I, who not only wanted to go as far south as possible but wanted to go all the way, have no regrets."

The *Resolution* returned. Cook was right. Nowadays we know that the 'Southern Land' offers nothing but dreary wastes of land, covered by ice and snow.

Returning to New Zealand by a route that took him to the mysterious Easter Islands, the Tonga Islands, the New Hebrides and New Caledonia, he then set out to make one final survey of Antarctica, to confirm his earlier observations, and at last headed back to Britain, where he dropped anchor on 30th July, 1775.

He felt convinced that no man could have done more to explore the Southern Pacific, and the acclaim with which his findings were greeted showed that his country agreed. More satisfying than anything to Cook, however, was that in more than three years at sea, he had lost only four men.

By 1776—now famous, and promoted to Captain—he was back at sea once more on yet another voyage of discovery and exploration. This time his orders were to explore the North and, in particular, to seek a passage from the Pacific to the Atlantic—the famous North-West Passage that so many had talked about.

His *Resolution*, accompanied this time by the *Discovery*, headed first for Cape Town, tacked across to Tasmania and New Zealand, and from there onwards to Tahiti, where he was greeted warmly again by the natives.

It was a welcome thoroughly deserved, for one of the admirable things about James Cook was that he always treated the many new peoples he encountered with the utmost respect. Never once did he order hostilities against them, however wild they seemed.

Leaving Tahiti, the two ships ventured out into the Pacific, and quite by chance stumbled across an unknown archipelago —today's Hawaiian Islands.

It was said that the Spanish had discovered the islands two centuries before, but to Cook . . . "it was obvious that these people had never seen Europeans before, nor had they ever heard of the conquests of our civilisation."

Fascinated by this unexpected discovery, Cook badly wanted to begin systematic exploration of the islands. But, as usual, he followed his orders, heading north in February, 1778.

Up to the north-west coast of America he sailed, navigated his way through the fog-shrouded Aleutian Islands, and finally in August headed through the Bering Strait, virtually unknown waters at that time.

Life aboard the ships was hard and cold, the men grew restless as they were heaved to and fro by the stormy, freezing seas in which formidable icebergs kept looming out of the mists.

Imperturbable, Cook kept the ships going forward through ever increasing ice until he reached 70° 41′ North. And finally he called enough. His chances of sailing much farther were very remote, he knew, and even if there were a North-West Passage, he certainly wasn't going to pass through it, for it would be blocked by ice.

His mind turned to the Hawaiian Islands once again. He suspected their importance, and meant to identify and explore them more fully.

By November, 1778, he was back there, sailing among them, constantly taking positions, making reliefs, drawing maps until in January, 1779, he finally gave orders to land and study the islands and their people themselves.

The two ships dropped anchor in the Bay of Kealakekua, and within days the crews had almost forgotten the hardships of their northern voyage, so overwhelming was the wonderful beauty around them.

Their contentment was marred only by the hostility of the natives, who occasionally attacked them as they were collecting supplies. But Cook was not too worried by this, for he had always got on quite well with other inhabitants of Pacific islands. He felt he could clear up any misunderstandings as soon as he had the opportunity to get ashore himself.

On 14th Frebruary, however, still working, he was suddenly disturbed by the sound of a musket shot. Before long, an officer entered his cabin to report another skirmish with the islanders. Knowing his captain's views about the use of violence, he had to admit that one of the men had opened fire while being pursued, and had killed a native.

His return to Tahiti was welcomed warmly by friendly islanders, happy to see him again.

Rather annoyed, Cook went up on deck and asked for a boat to take him ashore. The beach was crowded with gesticulating islanders, all shouting at the sailors who nervously held their muskets at the ready.

Calmly, their captain walked past his men, into the throng of natives and looked about for their chief. There was a stunned silence. But only for a moment. Suddenly another skirmish started on the beach behind him and more shots were fired.

"Quiet!" shouted Cook, swinging round towards the beach. "Stop that fire!"

And at that same moment, an islander leapt at him, crashing down a stone on his head. Even as he fell, another islander stabbed him in the back. Without a cry, James Cook toppled forward, his glorious voyages ended forever.

Many of his crew died with him that day in the massacre that followed on the beach, before the others rowed hastily back to the ships.

It was a terrible tragedy. Many empty spaces had been filled on the maps of the world by James Cook. The space left by his death among the greatest sea-faring explorers would never be filled.

RÉNÉ CAILLÉ

Réné Caillé could expect one of two fates
if he did not achieve his epic aim . . .
swift and sudden death by the sword or slow,
lingering death in a cruel wilderness

As the Sahara sun was setting, the shadows of dusk closing in, a young Frenchman, limping badly, stumbled into an oasis and sat down thankfully, his back against the first palm tree he saw.

Not for a moment would anyone have suspected that 28-year-old Réné Caillé was a Frenchman. His face was bronzed, he wore the long, flowing robes and headdress of an Arab, and he had adopted many Arab mannerisms.

Breathing heavily after a day's exhausting march across the burning sands, he stared for a moment at the festering wound in his foot, shrugged, reached for the paper, ink and quill he carried and began writing notes on top of the open pages of the Koran, the holy scriptures of the Arabs.

Suddenly he was aware of a figure standing over him. Glancing up, he found himself looking into the suspicious eyes of a fierce Arab, glaring down at him menacingly.

"What are you doing?" the Arab demanded, peering more closely. "What is that you are writing?"

"I am translating the word of the prophet into the language of the unfaithful," replied Réné as calmly as he could. But his heart was pounding as he spoke. If that Arab could read any French and even suspected that the young traveller was a white man making notes about his journey, all would be up. Réné Caillé's head would have been sliced from his shoulders with one sweep of a curved sword and his bones left to bleach in the sun.

But the Arab grunted. seemed satisfied with the reply and walked away to join his feasting companions, other travellers on a caravan making its way to Kambaya, a town buried deep in the African interior, a town that to Réné Caillé was an important stepping stone on the way to his ultimate goal— Timbuktu, the legendary city which no white man was allowed to see on pain of death.

Réné Caillé had but one obsession in life and that was to become the first white man ever to set foot in that forbidden city and live to tell the tale. So far, so good, but the strain was beginning to tell, and more than once Réné wondered if he would ever see his own people again.

If he didn't, it was unlikely that anyone would miss him.

To put it brutally, he was little more than a nobody, loved and respected perhaps only by his family and a few friends, and even they thought he was rather crazy.

Born on 19th November, 1799, in a tiny French village called Mauze, Réné Caillé could never have said he had been blessed by fortune. The son of a humble apprentice miller, who had been falsely accused of robbery and sent to prison, Réné and his family had been subjected to scorn and shame by their neighbours; and, worse, forced to live in dire poverty.

His one real pleasure in life was reading, which he had learned only with the greatest difficulty. One book in particular, which came into his hands quite by chance, fascinated him above all others and bred the earliest ambition in his life. That book was *Robinson Crusoe*, and as soon as he had read it, Réné was fired with the desire to get away one day and travel.

From that time on, he read every travel book he could find— mostly borrowed, for he was too poor to buy any—and studied maps of the world until he almost knew them by heart. One country above all fascinated him. Africa. There were more blank spaces on the maps of Africa, it seemed to him, than any others. Fame or riches were just waiting there to be claimed, he reasoned in his daydreams. One day he meant to go to that land.

And so he did, when he was only sixteen. Having saved what to him seemed a fortune—sixty francs—he left his miserable little village without a single regret, and sailed as a cabin-boy aboard an Africa-bound ship. Réné didn't care to which part of Africa it was going. All he cared about was that he was on his way.

Disguised as an Arab, Réné plodded on across the burning Sahara.

L. ARCAS - 70

Senegal turned out to be its destination, and within weeks of landing Réné was on his first journey into the interior. It was a catastrophic trip. Ill-equipped in every sense, he was lucky to escape with his life, returning to the coast riddled with fever and forced to return to France to regain his health.

But the experience failed to destroy his dream. If anything, his resolve was hardened. One day he would return to that continent.

Several years passed before that day came, but in 1824, young Caillé set foot in Senegal again—and this time he had a definite aim in mind. This time his heart was set on getting to Timbuktu.

Few mysteries were more fascinating to the world at the time than the riddle of that city, buried for centuries deep in the desert, surrounded by glittering but obscure legends.

It had been visited in the Middle Ages by Benedetto Dei, a merchant from Florence, who had said that even cloth manufactured in Lombardy was to be found in its magnificent markets.

In 1500, an Arab traveller, Mohammed al-Wassen had written, "The town is filled with merchants and artists. There are great fountains. It has markets rich with cattle and cereals. The king travels on big camels, with an escort of 3,000 mounted soldiers. Scholars and scientists live there, and the king pays for them to study. And there are mosques with golden domes, and palaces and libraries filled with precious manuscripts which cost much money."

To Réné it sounded like some vision from the *Arabian Nights* —and he knew he would know no peace until he had seen that vision.

Poor, badly educated, not especially healthy and an indifferent conversationalist, he had only his sense of purpose to drive him on. But of one thing he was certain; he must rid himself of his appearance as a white man before he could even start his journey.

He started to live among the Arabs, learning to speak, write and dress like them. He learnt the Koran by heart, and he became more and more tanned until he actually looked like an Arab.

To avoid embarrassing questions, he claimed that he was an Egyptian, who had been kidnapped as a child by Napoleon's soldiers and taken as a slave to France. Now he had succeeded in returning to Africa, he would say, and wished to go back to his homeland.

At the same time, he kept asking for help from the French authorities, but the only assistance he was granted came from the British consul in Sierra Leone. Finally he got together 2,000 francs, and set out for Cacondy along the lower course of the River Nunez, and awaited the right moment to leave for his goal.

Only a very short time before he actually set out, he received a great spur to his ambition. He learned that the French Geographical Society was offering a prize of 10,000 francs to the first white man to reach Timbuktu.

Using up a little of his money and playing on his pitiful story of the slave longing to reach his homeland, Réné at last persuaded some Arab merchants to let him join their caravan bound for Kambaya, buried deep in the African interior.

On 19th April, 1827, he set out, his hopes high and growing higher as the caravan advanced farther into the desert.

Standing over him was a fierce Arab, demanding to know what he was writing. It was a moment of life or death.

But before long, the agony started. Despite his rigorous preparation and training, Réné began to realise they were not enough. He found he could not keep up with the others who marched at a fantastic pace from dawn until mid-afternoon, when the heat was so atrocious that he could hardly place one foot before the other.

To add to his troubles, one of his feet, not properly covered, was cut open and within a few days was that festering sore, made worse by irritating sand and parasites. Sometimes he limped, often he crawled, and more than once he clung to the reins of a camel and let himself be dragged along. Several times he lost sight of the caravan entirely and had to make his own way across the desert, rejoining the others long after they had pitched camp.

Finally, on 10th May, he reached Kambaya and, having healed his foot as best he could, he took up his journey again, this time trying to reach the River Niger, which was said to pass Timbuktu.

If he thought the first part of his journey difficult, worse was to come. Haggard and thin, reduced to rags, utterly exhausted and without a franc to his name, he literally dragged himself

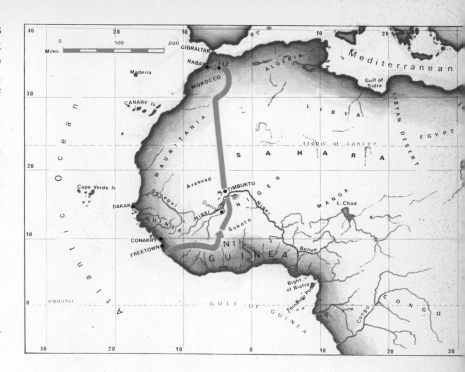

The craft sailed down the Niger, and among its cargo of slaves sat Réné Caillé.

He wandered in a daze of disbelief through the miserable town.

along the rough tracks said to lead to the Niger. When he stared down at his body, he saw with horror huge black spots that told him he had scurvy. More and more torturous his journey became. More than once he "implored God for death."

He very nearly did die, finally losing consciousness one day but coming to in a poor village near the Niger, where he had been taken by a band of Arabs who had stumbled across him. In the name of the Koran, which he knew by heart, he begged for hospitality which was granted him. Pitifully ill, he had to stay there for over six months before he could go on his way again.

Early in 1828, he set out once more, having been allowed aboard a craft, loaded with goods and slaves, that was making its way down the Niger. Only the charity of the slaves kept him alive this time, as they allowed him to share their meagre helpings of food. Spending long, torrid days and short freezing nights on deck, Réné travelled through magnificent scenery until 11th March when he was put off at Djenne, a remote village on the river.

Beyond some sand dunes, beyond a range of desolate mountains, he was told, lay Timbuktu.

On 20th April, exactly a year after his departure, Réné entered the forbidden city with a small caravan he had met. It was dead of night as they entered and the young traveller felt none too happy.

To his alarm, he had learned he was not the first white man to see the place, An 'infidel dog' had dared approach Timbuktu two years earlier and been killed, he was told. Later he learned the man was a Scotsman, Alexander Gordon Laing.

But Réné's enthusiasm still was undiminished. He waited sleeplessly for dawn to break. Soon the sun would be blazing down on the splendour of Timbuktu.

Sometimes he fell in the sand, unable to continue.

Its first rays peeped into the tiny hovel Réné had found, and at once he was on his feet, hurrying into the streets for his first glimpse of magnificence.

He stopped, swallowed and stared round, unable to believe what he saw.

"There were only badly built houses, made of mud and sand," he wrote. "All around I could see nothing else but sand. There were a few miserable brick houses, some wretched towers, one dome, white with lime, a few skeleton trees, and not a single fountain. The drowsiness, the sluggishness, the sadness of the desert oppressed the dreary street. Not even the singing of birds was to be heard."

He wandered around in a daze, his finest dream shattered to fragments. There were no rich markets, no signs of wealth or opulence anywhere. Climbing a bare hill, he finally saw the whole of Timbuktu at his feet. It was as miserable and wretched as the desert that surrounded it.

But Réné did not let his disappointment get the better of him. Beautiful or ugly, splendid or miserable, it was still Timbuktu. Réné had reached his goal and learned its secret.

He stayed there about a fortnight. Calm by now, and aware that an explorer should not chase legends but record reality, he walked the streets and squares of Timbuktu, making brief and swift sketches. He gathered news about the weather, about commerce and about the inhabitants of the town. And he witnessed one really splendid sight—the passage through the town of an enormous caravan from the south, its camels loaded with salt destined for all the villages and far-away oases of the Sahara.

On 4th May, 1828, he decided it was time he left. He had played his part of the returning Egyptian slave to perfection, but he could no longer stay without arousing suspicion.

Succeeding in joining a large caravan of about 1400 camels, heading north towards Tafilelt, he felt he might even accomplish something as important as his visit to Timbuktu—that is, become the first European to cross the Sahara from South to North.

His journey towards Kambaya had been swift and soul-destroying. His return journey to his own civilisation was slow and even more soul-destroying. Several times he learned again what it was like to hover on the verge of death. There were no wounds on his feet this time to torment him, no scurvy to eat away at his body, but there was a different kind of agony.

This time it was the indescribable heat of the sun, the slow plod through the burning, irritating sands and, most terrible of all, the dreadful torture of thirst.

By now, Réné looked like a beggar. In fact, he was one, living off the charity of other people who believed his continuing story of being an Egyptian escaped from slavery. He was given very little water—only those few gulps necessary to keep him alive. For sixty-four nightmare days, he staggered along roasting tracks. Thirst swelled his tongue, which filled his mouth like a gag, suffocating and torturing him. Any relief that water afforded him was offset by the dreadful effort of swallowing it. Fever clutched at his body and set him trembling, a racking cough seemed to be tearing at his insides.

And yet, despite all this, whenever he had sufficient strength, Réné kept making notes and drawing sketches of his travels.

On 14th August, 1828, little more than a walking skeleton, Réné reached Fez, from there made his way to Rabat and finally reached Tangiers. There filled with renewed enthusiasm—eager to tell the world he had seen Timbuktu and actually crossed the Sahara—he hurried to the French consul, forgetting entirely his appearance.

Covered with rags and coughing, having grown old, blackened, and in beggar's dress, he presented himself, a grotesque figure who seemed to have appeared from nowhere. But he was welcomed warmly by the consul who was "happy he had been the first Frenchman to embrace him."

Returning to his homeland at last, Réné was showered with the honours he deserved and the promised prize of 10,000 francs. Europe listened in amazement as he revealed the truth about Timbuktu in his lectures.

In place of the poverty and shame he had left behind in France, Réné now had considerable comfort and esteem. He settled down to write up his notes, which served as invaluable guides to future travellers, and he lived happily in La Badere until 17th April, 1838.

Ten years after he had entered the forbidden city, Timbuktu finally took her revenge for his daring invasion of her privacy. Réné died of the tuberculosis he had contracted on his glorious journey there and back.

Réné's return was slow and soul-destroying, tortured as he was by the glaring sun, his tongue swollen by thirst.

ROALD AMUNDSEN

He Conquered The South
But Yearned Only For The North

Rain, lashing like a whip, had emptied the seafront. Only the ships, seen bobbing at anchor in the reflected light from the water, remained. Their crews, sheltering from the storm, huddled in waterfront bars, listening to the tossing waves and the wind in the wire rigging.

Suddenly, in the centre of the tempest at Kristiania—where modern Oslo stands today—a ship moved in the harbour and, running up sail, made towards the open sea. At her helm, regardless of the rain, stood a tall, bearded man, his thin body taught with anxiety.

Every few moments the oilskin clad figure cast back anxious looks over his shoulder. He looked first at his crew of six, all straining to hear his every urgent whispered command. Then his eyes scanned the slowly receding harbour for any sign of activity that suggested his departure had been spotted.

But, bobbing and rolling, the tiny, 47-ton sailboat *Gjoa* rode the heaving sea safely that night of 16th June, 1903—and soon the harbour lights of Kristiania seemed little more than winking pinpricks on a dark and distant horizon.

For the first time, her skipper's lithe frame relaxed. The lines on his face turned to crinkles of pleasure and a sparkle lit up his eyes.

"At last," he smiled to his companions. "We are safe at last." The other six straightened from their tasks and grinned back broadly, sharing their leader's pleasure.

Strictly speaking, Roald Amundsen had committed theft that storm-tossed night. Ashore, he knew that one man in particular would be pacing the floor in fury, clenched fists crunching angrily, threats of dire revenge on his lips.

The man wanted money from Amundsen—money that he had loaned the adventurous Norwegian to equip and rig the small *Gjoa*. And when those debts had not been repaid in time, when every excuse had run out and each promise to pay had been broken, the exasperated creditor had decided to confiscate the ship.

That was why Roald Amundsen and his dedicated crew had made their do-or-die bid for the open sea. Had they not, the ambitions and hopes of a lifetime might have been shattered for ever.

It was no pleasure cruise they were set on making. What had called them to the open sea was a quest for knowledge and an irresistible inspiration to do things no man had done before.

First they meant to chart and scientifically study the challenging regions around the magnetic North Pole. Then they had set their minds to solving a problem that had fascinated every sailor, trader and explorer for centuries—finding the North-West passage, the Arctic waterway that links the Atlantic with the Pacific.

To achieve such things at all would be marvellous. To attempt to achieve them in such a tiny craft as theirs would be near miraculous.

Amundsen ploughed his way on with the dogged determination of a man inspired and dedicated. Beneath the *Gjoa* lay black, freezing Arctic waters which could solidify a man in moments. Looming up through swirling mists were mountainous cliffs and drifting ice floes. And always there were the storms and squalls that shook the rigging with frenzied violence and tossed the ship like matchwood in a tempest.

There were other hazards, too. Near the west coast of Greenland and the unknown waters of Peel Sound, the *Gjoa* and all her crew were almost destroyed when a fire broke out in the engine room. It was extinguished with only moments to spare.

Amundsen and his intrepid adventurers succeeded in the first part of their goal. In September, they found shelter from the violent westerly gales in a safe harbour which they named Gjoahavn. There they stayed for nearly a year, while Amundsen collected scientific data about the magnetic North Pole.

The Fram had made her way into Whale Bay. Soon the explorer was preparing for his race South.

On 12th August, 1905, the *Gjoa* set sail again, this time on the great, challenging adventure—to penetrate the North-West passage to the American continent.

Onward, ever onward, they sailed from Baffin Bay, edging slowly, carefully through the Bering Strait. From time to time, members of the crew had to lower a boat and take depth-soundings ahead of the ship. At one spot, there was only an inch of water to spare beneath their keel.

For thirteen days they sought their precarious course. Like a gaunt sentinel, sinews straining, spirits never sagging, Amundsen stood at the helm—watching and watching. At last he saw the sight that gladdened his heart.

"Ship ahoy!" The cry cut like a sabre through that chill morning on 26th August. Ahead was a whaling vessel, the American *Hansson*. The *Gjoa* was through. Amundsen had discovered the North West Passage.

Fortune was with them as they sailed through the Ross Barrier, usually blocked by ice.

It was surely the greatest moment of his life so far—a life he had dedicated to exploring the lonely and icy ends of the Earth. Yet even greater moments awaited this dauntless Norwegian.

What is it that makes such a man? What inner fires are kindled to make a human being drive body and soul to the conquest of the apparently unconquerable? What made Roald Amundsen more than just any ordinary man?

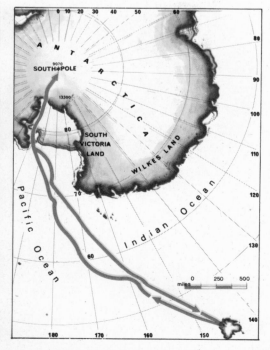

Borge is a fairly small town, not too far from Oslo, and it was there that Amundsen was born on 16th July, 1872. There was nothing extraordinary about his boyhood. His parents were as proud as any parents would be of a promising son. They hoped he would grow up to become a doctor, a wish that looked like being fulfilled when he enrolled at university to study medicine.

But it was not to medical books that young Amundsen turned his attention. On everyone's lips at the time was the name of Fridtjof Nansen, the great Norwegian Polar explorer. There were many tales about him—and all of them were read by Amundsen.

In 1893, in his specially built ship the *Fram*, Nansen drifted through the Arctic Sea in an attempt to reach the North Pole. Reaching 85° 57′, the most northerly point reached by man up to that time. He failed in his objective, but he reawakened a spirit of exploration and daring in men everywhere.

Certainly young Roald Amundsen was stirred by his earlier exploits. In 1889, Amundsen gave up his studies at University and went to sea as a cabin boy on a whaler.

Within eight years, he gained invaluable experience as a seaman and even qualified as a ship's captain—assets invaluable to a man so determined to master the polar seas.

Cruel, harsh and fearsome experience came in 1897 when, at the age of 25, he joined the *Belgica* as first mate. Commanded by a Belgian scientist, De Gerlache, the ship was to take an expedition beyond the Antarctic circle and spend a whole winter there.

It proved a viciously trying occasion for everyone.

Sailing by Cape Horn, they encountered nightmare gales of

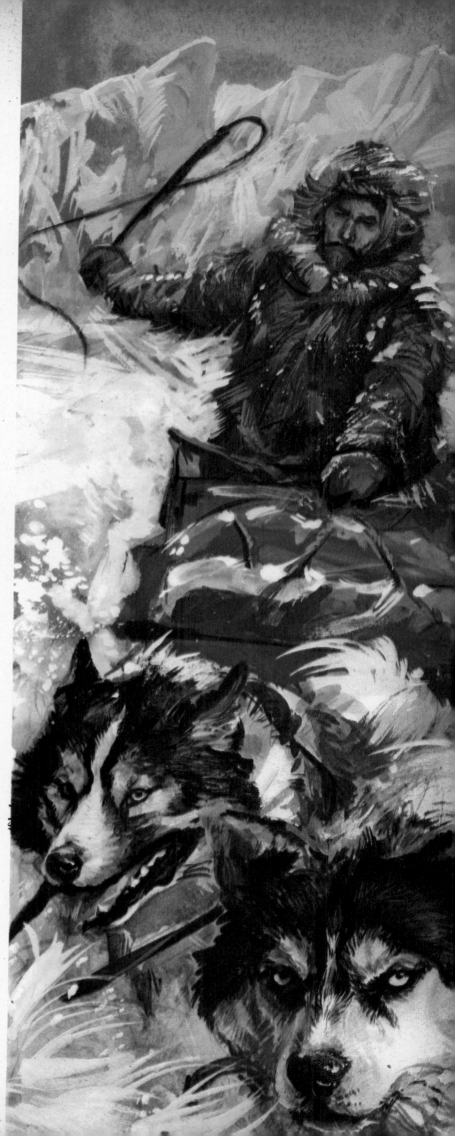

snow and sleet as they forged their way southwards. During one foul, ink-black night, the *Belgica* was driven between two icebergs, and in the morning mists the crew were shaken witnesses that only providence at her most charitable had stopped the frail hull of their ship being dashed to pieces.

Worse was to come. Only days after that perilous situation, the ship was trapped in the pack ice—where it remained, all but entombed, for thirteen months.

Then scurvy—that awful disease of the sea—swept the *Belgica*.

To Amundsen and the ship's doctor fell the task of nursing back the whole crew to health. And, in whatever spare moments were left to them, they kept up a vigilant search for some way out of the locking ice. Fortune smiled on them when they sighted a small basin of water about half a mile from the ship and felt convinced it led to the open sea.

The sick and weary crew hacked a channel towards it and negotiated the *Belgica* into the basin of water. From there they found a stretch that led to the open sea and freedom. Two years after her departure, the *Belgica* limped back into her home port.

Many of the crew vowed they would never again venture into those icy, heartless regions. Roald Amundsen made no such vow. If anything, his ambitions had been fired all the more.

What he wanted more than anything now was to lead an expedition of his own.

To where? The answer was clear. To the beckoning, mysterious 'roof of the world'—the North Pole.

During his epic voyage aboard the *Gjoa*—aboard which he earned undying fame as discoverer of the North-West Passage—he still dreamed often of emulating his hero Fridtjof Nansen, whose famous polar expedition had just fallen short of its goal.

It was to the famed old Norwegian hero that Roald went to seek advice. For long hours the two men talked, discussing how best this new claimant to that laurel crown of polar glory could achieve his end.

Slowly and carefully preparations were made. Roald hired Nansen's glorious old ship, the *Fram*, built expressly to withstand the enormous pressures of polar ice. A specially selected crew was signed on for the expedition. Each possible route was studied, its advantages and disadvantages considered thoughtfully. Dogs were selected to pull the sleighs on the final bid for the Pole. Finally, supplies were loaded aboard the ship.

The great adventure was about to begin.

Roald Amundsen sat in his cabin, his thoughts hovering over the glory that might soon be his. Scattered over his desk were reports of other explorers who had made the same brave bid to be first to the Pole. Suddenly there came a knock at the door.

"Come in!" called Amundsen. His first glance at the man who entered revealed something was wrong. The man's eyes were lowered and his voice was choked.

"Peary has got there," he said in a whisper.

At that moment clammy fingers clutched at Amundsen's stomach. His mouth was dry and his eyes were too vacant even to weep.

On 6th April, 1909, Robert Edwin Peary, the American explorer, had reached the North Pole.

What thoughts of bitter frustration and dismal heartbreak flowed and tossed through the mind of Roald Amundsen at that moment are anyone's guess.

To everyone's surprise, however, he ordered preparations for the voyage to go ahead as planned. Departure would take place

Coming back from the South Pole proved far easier than the journey to it.

Proudly the Norwegian flag
fluttered at the Pole.
Victory and glory
belonged to Amundsen.

on the day arranged, he said. Then Amundsen turned on his heel, walked back to his cabin and locked himself inside.

Day after day he stayed there, and the only man allowed to enter was his first officer, named Pestrud. Hour after long hour, Amundsen brooded over nautical maps and books and made sheets and sheets of notes. What on earth he was up to no one had any idea. In fact, it was unlikely that anyone even cared. The eyes of the whole world now were on Robert Peary. Thousands eagerly awaited news of the conquering hero's return, not the departure of the man who could at the most be second-best.

So there were no banners flying and few well-wishers as the *Fram* nosed her way out of Oslo and disappeared over the grey horizon. Indeed, why should there have been?

All that could be expected from Amundsen in the Arctic was perhaps some new scientific data; possibly one or two more interesting stories. And even if his expedition elected to head for the South Pole, what glory was awaiting there? Already Robert Falcon Scott and his British team were on the verge of conquering the last track of that unviolated world.

The *Fram* sailed steadily onwards, her destination a mystery to everyone aboard. Only when she was moored for a short stay in Madeira did Amundsen summon together his crew to address them.

"Gentlemen," he said, "we are not going to the North Pole. We are going to the South Pole."

Soon afterwards, Scott, who at the time was in Melbourne, Australia, with his expedition, received a short cable from the Norwegian explorer. "I am pleased to inform you that I am proceeding towards the Antarctic."

Amundsen had cast down the gauntlet. An enthralling challenge had been made. An exciting race was about to start.

Rapidly the news swept round the world. Two of the world's most respected explorers were to pit their courage against each other in a simultaneous bid to reach one of Earth's most formidable goals.

Legends about the South Pole were already plentiful. Many were the men—notably Shackleton and Scott—who had tried to reach it and failed. Protected by jagged crusts of ice, surrounded by seas said to be the stormiest in the world, those Southern wastes seemed contemptuous of man's puny attempts to gain a foothold there.

In his earlier attempt, Scott had driven himself to the limits of human endurance amid the icy Antarctic deserts, but still had been forced to surrender. Fearlessly, though, he had resolved to try for the Pole again, committed to give his every fragment of courage and effort to set the British flag on the white underbelly of the world.

And now he had a competitor for that honour—a man every bit as dedicated and determined as himself; a man equally courageous and committed; a man who had also known the despair of defeat when victory seemed within grasp; a hard and formidable Norwegian named Roald Amundsen.

Who—if either—would reach the South Pole first?

From Madeira, the *Fram* sailed steadily onwards, and soon it became apparent that Amundsen's expedition was to be blessed with the 'incredible good luck' he later described.

Whale Bay, to which they headed, was usually blocked with ice. But as the *Fram* nursed her way carefully forward, clear waters stretched all around, almost as if welcoming them inside the Ross Barrier, the gigantic natural monument of ice with which nature seems to defend the bleak continent.

Amundsen set up his base—which he named 'Framheim'—far from Scott's, which was many miles in the opposite direction at McMurdo Strait.

Now began the long weeks of preparation for the trek to the Pole. Nothing at all was to be left to chance. That hard teacher, experience, had schooled Amundsen that survival in the Antarctic could depend on the smallest things—badly repaired boots, frayed straps on skis, empty boxes of matches.

As the provisions and equipment were checked remorselessly, the men and dogs kept training without rest. Freezing cold, crustaceous ice, biting wind, driving snow, blanketing fog, glaring sun—nothing must take them by surprise. Every possible mishap had to be foreseen. Far too much was at stake for Amundsen and his hopes to be frustrated by clumsy or ill preparation.

Advance teams of the expedition had already pushed forward as far as latitude 82° South—and now Amundsen considered the moment ripe to make his bid for the real summit of achievement.

On 20th October, 1911, accompanied by four companions—Hansen, Hassel, Bjaaland and Wisting—he set out with four sledges and forty-eight dogs. Beneath a pale blue sky, they glided towards a white horizon and soon were lost from sight by the well-wishers at base.

Amundsen's plan of approach was straightforward. He had simply drawn a straight line from Framheim direct to the Pole and he meant to head straight along it.

At every degree of latitude, supplies of food were stored under well-marked heaps of ice—all of them needed for the return journey. Amundsen seemed far more concerned about the return trek than the epic push forward.

As the five men kept going, everything seemed too good to be true. The dogs strained and pulled eagerly to go forward, the morale of the men was at a peak, and the weather was holding well.

By the 17th November, they had reached 85° South, 163° East —and now Amundsen and his men left the Ross Barrier and headed into the frozen stretches of the Antarctic Continent. Though six of the dogs, too tired to press on, had to be put down, the men were still full of enthusiasm and there was still food in plenty.

But the landscape was changing now. Peaks of between 1,800 feet and 9,000 feet jutted up like mighty fangs, and many of them had to be climbed if the expedition was to stay on course. Skiing slowly, shouldering the sledges onwards and upwards, Amundsen and his men made ponderously slow progress. Flagging most of all were the labouring dogs.

Before 7th December—when they passed 88° 25′ South, the farthest point reached by the British explorer Sir Ernest Shackleton—twenty-four of the dogs had been put down and one of the sledges was beyond repair.

Then, suddenly, the weather began to worsen. White, wispy fogs started to swell and mushroom with menace, turning to heavy snow clouds that rushed like threatening chariots across the sky. Freezing winds howled and blew and bit into the bones, for a time even halting the expedition entirely. Snow came down like faceless packs of playing cards, burying the landscape beneath a mantle of white powder.

Was this the beginning of the end? The men bit their lips and wondered. Amundsen blinked upwards.

"The Pole is near now," he said quietly.

Was it a feeling of intuition? Or were they just encouraging words to urge his men on? Whatever the case, each man gritted his teeth and called on hidden reserves to plunge farther forward next day.

As though at their bidding, the snow suddenly stopped—and the march resumed in the glaring, silent whiteness.

On 14th December, at 10 o'clock in the morning, Amundsen wrote, "The sky covered itself with clouds blown by a light south-east breeze; but the clouds were not thick and the sun appeared every now and then with its bright orb. The conditions of the ground had changed. Sometimes the sledges would glide forward with no trouble. Often, though, it was difficult to advance. Even that day, the march proceeded automatically. We talked very little, but we observed a lot."

Above all, a great sense of expectancy hung in the air. Even the dogs, some of them limping and badly in pain, were yelping no more. Obediently they heeded their masters' calls and pulled bravely at the sledges.

Three o'clock in the afternoon came. And with every passing minute the intrepid explorers kept checking how far they had come. Every instrument was examined again and again. Surely the expedition was now not much more than a stone's throw from its objective? Yet again they checked to be entirely certain.

"Halt!" The command came at last. They didn't know whether to laugh or cry. The South Pole had been reached.

"I could not say," wrote Amundsen, "that I had the impression that I had reached the goal of my life, even if I know this phrase would have a very nice effect on the reader. If I wrote it, I would exaggerate. I want to be sincere, on the contrary, and confess that it is difficult for a man to find himself at the opposite end of his goal, as I was at that moment. Since I was a boy, the North Pole had exerted an enormous attraction on my spirit . . . but now I was at the South Pole. Nearer the antipodes than that I could not have been."

The five shook hands and slapped each other heartily on the shoulder.

"According to our calculations, we were at the South Pole. Of course, we knew that we were not exactly on the polar point. It would have been impossible to find it with the little time and the instruments at our disposal. But we were so near that point that to cover the short distance which still separated us from it did not matter."

Amundsen then took a bag from his sledge, pulled out the Norwegian flag and unfurled it.

"The eyes of everyone held a glimpse of pride and emotion when the flag opened at the freezing wind and fluttered over the pole. I had wanted the solemn act of raising the flag to be performed in such a way that everyone would feel part of it.

"Not just one of us, but every single one had to have this honour; all those who had risked their lives in the enterprise and had stayed united through all the dangers and hardships of the march. There, in that faraway and abandoned place, this was the only way to demonstrate my gratitude to my companions. I knew that they understood me."

All five of the fearless Norwegians then grasped the flagstaff and planted it in the snow and ice.

Proudly Amundsen wrote: "It was the first and only flag to flutter on the geographical south. Beloved flag. We plant you at the South Pole and we impose on the plain in which you are planted the name of the Land of King Haakon VII."

It was a very short ceremony. It had to be. Other things were more pressing.

Probably the saddest task of all was to kill one of the favourite dogs, so exhausted that it could go no farther. The poor animal "which had pulled the sledge from morning to evening without ever rebelling" was killed and fed to its companions.

Next the five men checked their sledges and decided that Bjaaland's would remain there as a kind of monument.

A tent was raised, and in the evening—while nothing was to be heard but the flapping of the flag in the wind—Amundsen and his men celebrated their victory "not with a bottle of champagne, but with seal meat which we found excellent and restored us marvellously."

They talked about their epic trek, but even more of friends and families so far away in Norway. And on every object on which they laid their hands they engraved or wrote the words: South Pole.

Amundsen next wrote a letter which he addressed to Scott, his British rival whom he felt would reach the Pole sooner or later. With a little touch of irony he asked Scott to deliver to King Haakon of Norway another letter which he left under the tent.

Amundsen could not have imagined that this would cause only bitter pain to the already unfortunate Scott. Certainly he could not have foreseen that a month later the desolate zone through which he was passing was to be the stage for a terrible tragedy.

Scott and his companions did, in fact, reach the South Pole on 18th January, 1912—after a march made desperate by continuous storms—and on their disappointed journey back they died one after the other.

But for the Norwegians the return was even easier than the going. "It has been a walk," Amundsen wrote. "Our dogs brought us for most of the journey. It is so easy to go to the Pole."

Another page had been written in history. The name of Amundsen was inscribed on it triumphantly. For many men such a triumph, such a convincing conquest of challenge, would have been more than sufficient.

Instead, it served only to whet the appetite of Roald Amundsen. His hunger for exploration grew greater. Again it was to the North that his stern, far-looking eye stared.

That haunting boyhood dream of reaching the North Pole had lingered too long in his soul not to be satisfied. His every thought kept turning to the Arctic.

Again he toyed with the possibility of fitting out a ship that would drift as near as possible to the Pole. Raising funds for such an expedition proved difficult, but Amundsen eventually succeeded and supervised the construction of a new polar ship, the *Maud*. Its design was based on that of the famous *Fram*.

All was ready when suddenly the First World War broke out in 1914. Amundsen was forced to curb his impatience for four years until the cannons were once again silent.

With a crew of ten, the *Maud* headed northwards, and Amundsen must have hoped again for the 'incredible good luck' that had blessed his successful Antarctic expedition to the South Pole.

By the end of 1918, he had his first suspicion that his good fortune had this time deserted him. Near the island of Celiuskin, the *Maud* was trapped like a manacled prisoner in thick ice—and there she remained for over a year before she managed to force herself free.

Then, within a few days, she was grasped in the vice-like ice once more, this time near the island of Ajon. Not until July, 1920, did she see the open sea again, after which her fearless captain decided to take her through the freezing waters of the North-East Passage to the port of Nome in Alaska.

There Amundsen gave leave to his crew. But he allowed himself no respite. With three friends, he again attempted to be drawn along by the drift. Again it was in vain. So much so that the Norwegian decided he would now make a bid for the Pole by plane.

Could any man have had an unluckier expedition than this one? Damaged in a preliminary test, the plane failed even to get off the ground. Amundsen's spirits reached their lowest ebb.

Seven years after her departure, the *Maud* limped back to Norway, to be greeted by only an indifferent and embarrassed silence. Even though a good deal of valuable scientific data had been collected, it was no consolation to Roald Amundsen. Nor did it win any public acclaim.

This time the Arctic had won. Bitterly disappointed, and riddled with debts, Amundsen felt the prospect of further enterprises was remote.

As it was, help came from an unexpected source. A young American millionaire named Lincoln Ellsworth placed his enthusiasm, his encouragement and—most important—his money at the Norwegian explorer's disposal.

Amundsen, who still dreamed of reaching the North Pole by air, went to Italy and bought two Dornier Waal Hydroplanes, both fitted with two 360 horse-power engines. In the spring of 1925, they were ferried from Marina di Pisa to King's Bay, Haakon Land in North-West Svalbard. And there they were put through their tests for the nearly 800 mile flight, expected to last between eight and ten hours.

As had happened so often before, everything now depended on the mercy of the elements. Repeatedly bad weather grounded the planes for days—until the morning of 21st May, when Amundsen finally took off.

As the two hydroplanes neared latitude 87° 44', the great unfriendly North stubbornly cast its unfriendly eye on Amundsen again. An enormous storm raged and drove the planes off course.

Short of petrol, they were forced down on the half-frozen sea, where one plane was damaged beyond repair. Again Amundsen knew what it was to be a prisoner of the ice.

Only after 27 days of hard, hurried work were Amundsen and his men able to take off in the remaining plane and fly towards Svalbard, where they were picked up by a whaler.

Again everyone—scientists, explorers and the public—was disappointed. The Pole, it seemed, could not be reached from the sky. And no one was more dejected than Amundsen.

Then, even while Amundsen was making preparations for another flight, the news arrived that American aviator and explorer, Richard Evelyn Bird, had taken off from King's Bay in a three-engined plane and flown over the Pole. For the second time in his career, Amundsen's attempt to win a 'first' from his hypnotic Pole had been frustrated by an American.

He took the blow well. But surely, it was thought, he would now start thinking of retirement. Had not fate as good as said to him that he and the North Pole were never to make each other's acquaintance?

Nothing of the sort, replied Norway's indomitable hero. He would yet fly across the Polar cap—but not in a plane. This time his attempt was to be made in an airship, which he declared was particularly suitable for polar exploration.

The airship which Amundsen was able to buy, thanks again to the help of the generous Ellsworth, had been built in Italy to a design of Colonel Umberto Nobile who, it was agreed, would take part in the enterprise as captain of the airship. There were also to be five Italian mechanics aboard when the

Norge—as it was called—left for the North Pole.

The flight started from Rome on 10th April, 1926, and the *Norge* reached King's Bay on the 7th May. Four days later, in a clear, blue sky, it soared towards its goal.

Perfect was the only word to describe the journey. At 1.30 p.m. on 12th May, three flags—Italian, Norwegian and American—were dropped from the sky on to the North Pole. At long last, Amundsen had realised the dream of his life.

For a long time he stayed glancing down at the wide expanses of the world's roof, while the *Norge* floated on towards Alaska, cruising its way over zones that had never been seen before. Fighting storms of wind and ice, the airship finally reached the base at Teller after 71 hours travel.

It was a classic triumph—and Amundsen was full of himself.

Sadly, though, it was also the beginning of a long controversy.

Already there had been misunderstanding between Amundsen and Nobile before and during the enterprise. And now the flight of the *Norge* was over, someone asked who had been the actual conqueror of the North Pole.

Was it Amundsen, whose idea it had been all along? Or Nobile, who had piloted the airship? The controversy seemed never-ending and inconclusive.

In 1928, Nobile left Milan in an airship similar to the *Norge*. It was called the *Italia* and it was clear to everyone that the young Italian officer intended to take revenge on the hardened old Norwegian explorer. Obviously he meant to undermine the glory of Amundsen once and for all.

Soon after the flight of the *Norge*, Amundsen had retired to his house in Borge. His greatest wish had come true. The one big aim of his life had been attained. Now he intended to say farewell to his explorations, to end his adventurous life amid memories.

But fate was to call him once more to the Arctic.

At 0.20 hours on 25th May, 1928, Nobile's *Italia* reached the Pole, but only a few hours later it crashed on to the ice pack.

Some of the crew were hurled to the ground. Others remained trapped in the airship's cabin and vanished forever as the *Italia* bounced off the ice and soared again into the air and oblivion.

All Nobile and the other survivors could do was await help in a small tent, hoping against hope that the world would rally to their assistance. It did. Ships and planes from many nations volunteered to go to the assistance of the stranded men. And among the searchers was Roald Amundsen.

His differences with Nobile were now forgotten. All he had professed to care about was enjoying his retirement in Borge. But when the lives of men in the Arctic were in danger, Amundsen's experience was too valuable to be left at home.

On 18th June, 1928, the hard, strong, wrinkled, white-haired explorer climbed aboard the French seaplane of Captain Guilbaud, which took off from Tromso in Norway for Svalbard.

The seaplane, a Latham 47, circled, turned north towards the sea of Baerens and disappeared over the horizon. To this day no one knows what happened afterwards. No one came back, though part of the plane was found some time afterwards.

And so in a final supreme act of generosity, in one last magnificent challenge to the North Pole—to its fogs, winds and ices which had preoccupied him throughout his life—Roald Amundsen disappeared.

In the freezing waters of the Arctic he found probably the only tomb worthy of him.